JUSTICE
FOR
QADIRA

KARELLEN STEPHENS

ISBN: 9798577075651
Imprint: Independently published

DEDICATION:

This book is dedicated to THE TRUTH

CONTENTS

INTRODUCTION

- Qadira Stephens was a victim of child abuse by Todd Burkholder and Aimee McQuiston on April 12, 2007.
- She was burned with scalding water from a teakettle.
- She sustained 2nd and 3rd degree burns on 10-19% of her body.
- She was only 8 years old and 59 pounds.
- She was seen at Providence St. Vincent and OHSU hospitals.
- The Police and DHS were not notified.
- Her parents were sent home alone to care for her wounds.
- Her parents were told to go to the medical store and get bandages and silvadene.
- Her parents were given no appropriate supplies, medicine, instructions, or supervision of any kind.
- Qadira Stephens went into organ failure and almost died.
- Qadira Stephens lives with a host of compounding medical issues.
- Qadira Stephens and her family have suffered severe physical, mental, and emotional distress.
- The Portland Police Bureau, The District Attorney's Office, The Department Of Justice, and The Federal Bureau Of Investigation have all been notified and adamantly refuse to investigate or help in anyway.

THE UNCOMFORTABLE TRUTH

I don't know what you have heard but this is our story. In 2007 my family went through a series of shocking events. First my husband Renee was forced to complain about inappropriate conduct against a senior co-worker at Nike. Specifically and there is just no other way to put this so, if you have small children ask them to cover their ears. This man named Randy Wolfe that my husband used to work with must have lost his mind because he tried to dry-hump him on the job at the Nike World Headquarters.

There I said it. I REALLY, REALLY, REALLY needed to get that off my chest. And he did this after dry-humping and groping another senior co-worker named Cory McCullough right in front of my husband. Renee was not friends with either of the men outside of work but up until that point he had had a mostly cordial working relationship with both of them. My husband Renee is one of those super nice people who are well liked by just about everyone he meets and up until this point in his working career he had never encountered anything even remotely like this. It was a very intimidating circumstance. Nike was a place full of professionals and he had worked very hard to try and fit in.

So anyway to give you some context the two men I am talking about were white and in their early forties. They were both senior designers and the guy who was doing all the dry-humping and groping just happened to be my husband's supervisor. It was a very uncomfortable situation. Renee is Filipino and black and at twenty eight years old he just happened to be a spot of color in a sea of white faces on the Nike campus. The truth is Nike doesn't really hire very many minorities unless you want to count the thousands of slaves that they drive mercilessly in their overseas factories in Phil Knight's quest to "own" the world. If I sound a little disappointed with Phil then you must keep reading to understand my side of the story. But who am I to be talking about Nike co-founder Phil Knight? Because who am I? If you don't have a lot of money on this planet you might as well not exist, right? The level playing field is like Santa Claus which means it sure would be nice if it was real. It would certainly be great to live in a world where everyone was given equal opportunity but that was not this place. I still remember the night Renee came home and told me what had been happening.

My friend Haley is an athletic white girl with big curly hair and a loud voice and she just happened to be over visiting when Renee came in obviously tense and upset. "What's wrong?" We both asked. But he just shook his head and went immediately to the fridge to grab a beer. Haley and I looked at each other wondering what was up. It wasn't often that something could make Renee visibly upset and today was one of those days. Something must have happened at work.

His job at Nike could be pretty stressful at times. Maybe it wasn't the best night for company but I figured we could talk about what was bothering him later after Haley left. But as the night progressed and the alcohol hit his bloodstream he opened up and started telling us what had happened. I can't say how I felt when he started explaining what had been going on but I do remember Haley and me just kind of going silent and staring at each other like what did he just say?

I must admit it takes a lot for Haley and I to manage being quiet especially when we get together. But what was Renee talking about? I was literally thinking to myself did Renee just tell me that a grown ass man had dry-humped another grown ass man in front of him? Haley and I stared at each other for a moment like what the HELL did Renee just say? It just didn't sound right. This was obviously not okay. Renee worked at Nike and people up at Nike didn't act like that. I'm usually not at a loss for words but this time it was taking me a few minutes to respond.

My friend had whipped her big hair around and was staring at Renee with the most shocked expression on her face. Like what? She said "wait a minute, what What WHAT?" Each "what" got louder than the next. Haley had been raised with poise and manners in a solid middle class home in a world where these things didn't happen. There are just certain places and certain situations where certain types of behavior are just not acceptable. Certainly the Nike World Headquarters was one of those types of places. Haley had a working knowledge of how to behave in the world of the wealthy and what Renee was describing did not fit the description of what she was used to.

Haley and I had just recently reconnected when she moved back to Portland from California but we had been friends since forever. She had grown up right down the street from me. We had lost touch for several years but she had found me again still living in the old neighborhood right down the street from her parents. I was more than grateful to finally have a friend living nearby that I could hang out with and we would get together at least once or twice a week for drinks or dinner. The demographic of the neighborhood had changed while I was away and it wasn't exactly easy for me to connect with my neighbors. Having Haley around was making the transition back to the neighborhood a little bit easier.

In 2006 things for me had begun to get a little easier. The house was shaping up. I had finally lost all of the baby weight. Qadira and Kymani had gotten into The Odyssey Program at Hayhurst bringing with it the promise of a more interesting school year. The program was all based in Native American history and seemed to offer more diversity than the kids were getting at Maplewood which was our neighborhood school. Keeping our kids exposed to a more diverse environment was something of a priority for us since the neighborhood was so white and since Hayhurst was still basically walking distance from our house it was convenient.

Qadira's little friend Sophie whom she had become friends with in Kindergarten when we first moved into the house had also been accepted to the program, so they would be making the switch together which was nice. From the year Qadira had been born in 1998 to 2004 it had seemed that I had been perpetually pregnant and nursing. 4 kids in just a few short years had brought with it a load of constant adjustments and with limited resources I didn't have much time for myself much less friends. But 2007 was supposed to be our year. The kids were getting bigger and easier to manage and with Haley back in my life I was getting out into the world more. I was getting my wardrobe together, making plans to go back to school, and just in general feeling like more of a person instead of just a mom. Now Haley and I were sitting here in shock listening to my husband tell us an absolutely outrageous story.

THE NEIGHBORHOOD

It was in 2004 that Renee and I made the decision to buy my childhood home located in the hills of SW Portland. Raising kids can be very isolating and the neighborhood I grew up in had changed from working class to upper class. We knew we weren't going to fit in when we bought the place but Renee and I had reasoned that the house would be a good investment. This wasn't the type of neighborhood that young people of color typically had the opportunity to buy into. Real Estate agents are not supposed to discriminate but let's keep it real. They do it all the time. How else do some neighborhoods stay perfectly segregated?

Since we had the chance to buy the house from my mom we figured even if we didn't fit into the neighborhood we could fix up the house and eventually sell it for a nice profit. Something had to be done. My mom was in an impossible predicament. The house was in need of major renovations and repairs and she needed to sell it right away or risk losing it to foreclosure. It was built in 1912 so it was 92 years old when we purchased it and my mother had literally never done a repair she didn't have to do. Her life hadn't been easy. My dad had struggled with mental illness for years and she had been left to raise 6 kids all by herself so she never had time or money to do much of anything.

When my brother Sala was diagnosed with Bipolar Disorder following in my father's footsteps a few years after I graduated from high school, it brought with it a whole host of unforeseeable issues.

Eventually my mother had to quit her job as a Systems Analyst to try to help him deal with it. She just couldn't manage my brother and her job anymore. If you have ever had to deal with a family member suffering from mental illness then you know that there are really no good services or help for people with these types of conditions. Losing your mind on this planet usually means losing everything else you have which makes finding your mind a very low priority. Seriously people on this planet have little to no empathy for those who cannot cope. In fact the consequences of losing your mind are far greater when you find your mind again so there is very little incentive to want to get better.

In a world where you are judged like you don't belong for every little thing that you do it's not all that hard to find yourself wanting to stay checked out from society permanently. This was my brother. For him getting better meant feeling embarrassed about being sick in the first place and who wants to do that? It also meant having to rejoin the "rat race" which is what caused the problem in the first place. The chains of conformity can be just tight enough to be uncomfortable but comfortable enough to wear. For those of us who are having trouble breathing in this chaotic society there are no good solutions. Breaking out of the chains means that things can never really go back to the way they were, but staying in them can kill you.

The truth is this world is a mess and even the most level headed individual can find themselves feeling incredibly confused and lost. Once diagnosed with a "mental illness" people are told that they are the problem not the world around them. Treatment is a host of pills to help you cope with our crumbling society; like somehow pills have the power to make this world a nicer place.

Whoever came up with the idea that you can cure something that is (in my opinion) purely environmental and circumstantial by manipulating the brain on the inside probably needs to have their head checked. So anyway now my brother was branded with the idea that there was something wrong with him. Even if he could learn to manage the disease the stigma of having it would never go away. In our society mental illness is one of "those" diseases. You know "those" we do not speak of.

And if people do find out what you are dealing with they don't exactly feel bad for you like they do than if you have something like cancer. You know something that isn't your fault. Because it's kind of like it's your fault for not being able to cope. And when family members acquire the new job of taking care of their mentally ill loved one it is not considered "work" by society. Most jobs that involve taking care of life on this planet are not associated with making very much money or any money at all, so people just do not appreciate how hard they can be and they don't care.

People are usually left all alone managing the compounding stress unless they can pay someone to help them, and sometimes that's not even enough depending on what the person you are now paying has going on. Anything can happen and the consequences are always very real. And it sure felt like a whole bunch of extra work and stress to my poor mom when she was sitting at her "real job" worried about what was going to happen while she was away. Every single day can bring a major disaster. We never knew what my brother might do next and my mom was shouldering the brunt of this new "burden" living with him.

I had moved out with Renee at the age of 18 but I was always running over to help my mother when I could. There could be daily emergencies. Sala threatening to kill himself, Sala threatening my mother, threatening to burn down the house, freaking out listening to the voices in his head, peeing and pooping in buckets and not coming out of his room for days on end. It was exhausting for everyone involved.

He was in and out of the hospital and on and off different medications. One year he took to exclusively wearing dresses. He was quite a sight to behold with his bald head and Birkenstocks and he would go all over town dressed like this. It could be pretty embarrassing but what could we do? If we wanted him to survive he needed daily family support from anyone who was willing to give it.

I always did what I could to help. If that meant talking to him over and over multiple times a day then so be it. When I finally secured a loan to buy the house it was not only in need of repair but it was a mess. Sala and his illness had done a number on the place and my mother's hoarding condition hadn't helped. The house was in shambles. There were holes in the walls, no electricity in certain rooms, rotting floors and cabinets, writing on the walls. This was going to be a huge undertaking. But in 2003 my mother had gone into business with my sister running an adult foster care home for the elderly called Benchview Place and she needed out.

They had bought the place from my brother Uranus and his wife at the time who were both desperate to unload the business and make a fresh start in an attempt to fix their failing marriage. Both my mom and sister had already been helping out at Benchview so buying the place was a natural progression. My mom was finally moving on and she just couldn't deal with the house or my brother anymore. She had to go back to work. Her retirement had dried up and she had run out of money.

Benchview was a 24 an hour 7 day a week operation and she was hardly ever even home anymore. Even I started working there on the weekends. Unfortunately for my mother in order to put my two older sisters Urania and Leyenda, and my brother Soni through college she had continued to borrow against her house. She now owed 3 times what she bought the place for. It was going to be hard to get someone to buy the house for what she owed especially in the condition that it was in. It was a rock and a hard place because nobody in the family wanted to see the old house foreclosed on.

We all felt that would be a terrible shame. My mom had worked really hard to buy that house. It was in a really good neighborhood where home values were continuing to go up so even in the condition that it was in it carried with it the promise of opportunity. Renee and I weren't exactly looking to take on a project but back then we were young and optimistic. We lived in a world of endless possibilities. We believed his career at Nike was going well and even with our 4th child on the way we believed that we could buy that house and fix it up to.

My neighbors were friendly but they were all older, white, and well established. There was a heavy Jewish presence due to our close proximity to "Everything Jewish" in Portland. And I mean that literally. It was the name of a small boutique not far from our house right across from the Jewish Community Center. I guess this had always been the case even when I was growing up but I was more aware of it now. Things were a little awkward to say the least but we were determined to make it work. When we bought the place Sala took to living in his van mostly staying parked on the side of the house. Of course it didn't help our reputation to have my "crazy" brother basically living in a van on the side of my house but that was my brother so what could I do?

He was harmless but boy could he be irritating especially in the middle of everything that we were dealing with. Thankfully the neighbor's never said anything to us but I am sure they noticed. I guess technically nothing had really changed all that much. My mother was white but none us kids were. Our family had lived on the corner for years so when Renee and I moved our family into the house it was just one loud brown family replacing the last loud brown family. The tradition was set to continue. Some of the neighbors I already knew from my childhood so we kind of had a small buffer but there were also a lot of new faces to contend with.

We tried to make a good impression. We cleaned the place up remodeling as much as we could. We had purposely purchased the place for as much as the bank would loan against it so we could make the much needed repairs. It had been very difficult to make that happen but it was the only way we could have agreed to buy the place. My mom had agreed to give us just enough money from the proceeds of the sale of the house to do the basic repairs she had neglected over the years.

It was going to be an enormous stretch. Renee did as much as he could by himself learning as much as he could from most of the contractor's that we hired. For a while he literally worked night and day going from our apartment to Nike to the house sleeping only a few hours a night when he was trying to get the house ready for us to move into it after the close of the sale. When we finally moved in our neighbors were welcoming. Our kids made friends with the neighbor kids and they all played nicely together. Things were going a little better than expected but we still felt out of place in our new environment.

When I was a kid my brothers and sisters and I were the only children of color in the neighborhood but at least we weren't the only ones who struggled financially so I think that made things a little easier socially. Back then it was Haley's family that had been considered one of the wealthier families in a solidly middle class working neighborhood. I remember being a little jealous of her perfectly clean house and fashionable clothes but that wasn't the kind of money I was encountering now. This was different.

By the time Renee and I bought the house a new kind of money had taken over the neighborhood. I certainly couldn't refer to my neighborhood as solidly middle class anymore. In 2004 tiny little houses were being sold for astronomical prices and people were buying. If a contractor had gotten their hands on my mother's property they probably would have knocked the place down and replaced the old house with something brand new. A decent sized new build in our area could easily run the buyer a half a million dollars.

The face of the neighborhood had slowly been changing. In place of the neighbors that I grew up with who had been grocery clerks, laborers, salesman, and stay-at-home moms there were now professionals who did professional things. They were teachers, lawyers, engineers and businessman. They shopped at New Seasons and their children had "play-dates" and were carted around in strollers long after they could walk. They had wine and cheese parties and sent their dogs to daycare and when they went walking in the evening they wore reflective vests.

It was a different world and I couldn't help but feel inadequate. I didn't know where I fit into this puzzle and it was now my home. Renee and I were just both high school graduates with 4 kids in tow. At least Renee worked at Nike; at least we could say that. That always made us feel better. It was like our badge of honor. It was the "something" that said we belonged where we were.

When Haley reappeared in my life I was grateful because she hadn't changed much and since she was a nanny she was used to being around kids so she didn't mind all of mine. Her father had worked very hard as a salesman to provide for their family and her parents had expected her to work hard and make her own money. Even though she wasn't married with kids we still had a lot in common and it was nice to have a friend living nearby that I could relate to.

Like most Americans her parents had instilled in her the value of The American Dream and like Renee and I she was busy chasing it the only way she knew how. In the game of survival she had been a nanny for as long as I could remember. She worked for wealthy families like the kind of people who worked at Nike. Upper class white professionals who didn't act the way Renee was describing. We were both captivated by what he was telling us.

THE WHOLE STORY

I was quick to ask the first question. I wanted to know what Cory had done when Randy had jumped on him. Renee said that Randy had been very aggressive with Cory pounding on his backside with 7 or 8 hard thrusts. It was very disturbing. The first time he witnessed this Cory hadn't said a word. On another occasion when Randy groped Cory he had chopped his hand hard up in between the crevice of Cory's buttocks and then he squeezed hard. Renee had stood by thinking to himself "that must have hurt." It looked painful but still nobody said anything.

Cory had just stood there with a strange expression on his face that wasn't pleasure or amusement. Renee didn't know what to do so he just walked away. "What was I supposed to do?" He wondered aloud. Haley and I didn't have any answers because we were still trying to make sense of what he was saying. The story he told us was so SHOCKING that our minds were still trying to process what he had been saying. I mean this had happened at Nike? And that's when Renee started telling us what Randy had tried to do to him.

Randy and Cory were in the storage room taking inventory of the Starter samples. Renee had a question about a tech pack that he was working on and he entered the storage room to ask Cory and Randy what to do. They both ignored him and Randy put on a workout jacket and pretended he was warming up for a run. Renee stood by patiently waiting for Randy to finish what he was doing. Then suddenly Randy grabbed Renee around the waist and tried to dry-hump him. Renee was prepared for what Randy was going to do because he had seen him do it to Cory. He quickly executed a move that he had learned from his 3 years of Tai Chi and was able to ward Randy off.

He firmly told Randy that he wasn't going to do that to him. Randy got right back up in his face and said he would try it again when he was thirty. Was that a threat? Cory just stood there watching the interchange without saying a word. Renee told Randy again that he wasn't going to be doing that. Randy said to him "You're too virile of a young man to not have tried sleeping with another man." Renee firmly informed him that he would never do that and he left the storeroom. He felt weird and uncomfortable and he went immediately back to his desk to gather his thoughts. His feeling was if Cory was going to let Randy to that to him then that was Cory's decision but he was not going to let Randy do that to him.

I was having difficulty seeing where Cory fit into all this? Did Cory welcome Randy's advances? Was Cory somehow involved in what Randy was doing? I was aware that both Randy and Cory were married so things weren't exactly adding up. Why do this at work in front of other people? It appeared to me that even if they were having some kind of affair Randy's actions still didn't seem right. But maybe this was their way of propositioning Renee? I don't know. Maybe Randy was just losing his mind?

I had met Cory on two occasions. The first time was at the office when I was just passing through with Renee. He had worn a light pink long sleeved button up with the top button undone and light colored slacks. He had a soft polite voice and cordial demeanor. He was not unlike a lot of the people that I had met at Nike over the years. You know the type. Clean cut, well-manicured, and spoon fed from day one. In my mind Nike definitely had a type and Cory fit the description. The second time I had a chance to meet him was at a company dinner at The Chart House where I also had the chance to meet his wife Irene who was openly disappointed when Randy didn't show up. She also wanted to know who had the nerve to be calling themselves "Big Daddy" at work. Randy had quite the little reputation. I had never met him so I couldn't put a face to the name either but I imagined him to be kind of like Cory.

As the night wore on and Renee loosened up he divulged that there had been other incidents before all of this. I knew that Randy had been getting under Renee's skin for some time but I had no idea what had really been going on. On one occasion Randy had pulled his pants down in front of Renee and bent over a table and asked him to "start mounting." And there was the time Renee had been standing at Randy's computer and Randy had lifted up the back of Renee's shirt to glance at his butt. Renee was extremely uncomfortable but he just kept walking away and pretending that nothing was going on.

Then there was also the time that Randy had asked Renee in front of a young female intern named Afton Walsh what man Renee would sleep with. Randy openly proclaimed his preference for Pierce Brosnan. Renee firmly told Randy he wasn't having that conversation and walked away again. And then there was the FULL ON SHOCKER! Something to this day I still cannot quite comprehend. Ladies and Gentleman straight from The Book of You Can't Make This Shit Up, drumroll please......... The second and last time when Renee witnessed Randy dry-humping Cory, Cory said "I can feel your little Elvis." So there you have it folks this was not your everyday situation. Something was all the way wrong.

Haley and I both felt very strongly that Renee should complain immediately and we both encouraged him to do so. I mean I expected Renee to work but I didn't expect him to have to put up with that. Haley and I were both sure that Nike would want to know about this. Randy was obviously out of control and needed some kind of mental help. Nike was a world class company with standards. In fact when it came to harassment they had a zero tolerance policy.

Obviously Renee needed to speak up. If this was supposed to be some kind of joke it wasn't funny at all. I had watched my husband struggle to climb the corporate ladder over the years. He was always looked over for a promotion and he had spent 10 years as a Color Designer 1. He had even designed some shoes for Nike that they made and sold but even then he was never acknowledged or promoted. But he had finally gotten his chance when Nike decided to break into the value market with a new subsidiary which they called Exeter Brands Group. He had put up with a lot to get where he was and he didn't need Randy ruining things for him now.

EXETER BRANDS GROUP

Exeter was initially created by Nike in 2004 to house Nike's new Starter Brand. But in March of 2007 the stars and moon were lining up and Exeter had signed Elton Brand to help market the Starter product and they were getting ready to launch the new Tailwind brand. They had signed a multi-year deal with Payless Shoe Source to be the exclusive retailer of the Tailwinds. Nike was literally poised to take over the value channel market with a new low cost high quality line of shoes.

Soccer stars Hope Solo and Brandi Chastain along with world renowned volleyball player Logan Tom were brought out to help launch the collection. The running shoes featured new Nike developed technology called the "G-Zone" which was a honeycomb gel that compresses on impact to cushion the heel. Tailwind's women's line had already rolled out to 400 Payless stores on February 26th and the entire collection was expected to hit all 4,600 Payless stores by the years end. This was just two days before Renee witnessed Randy dry hump Cory for the first time.

It was in 2006 that Skip Lei had offered Renee the position of Footwear Design 1. Skip was the grandfatherly type who had been at Nike forever and Renee was absolutely thrilled at his suggestion. Finally his dreams were coming true. He could barely contain his excitement. He was finally going to get a chance to start moving up. Now this wasn't exactly a promotion because although the job came with increased responsibility it did not come with much of a raise and they would certainly not be raising Renee's band level. Your band level indicated your value to the company and Renee was squarely on the bottom of the corporate rung. He had been on the bottom the entire time he worked at Nike.

After 8 years of near perfect reviews he sat waiting patiently at the bottom. But now along with his color work Renee would officially have the opportunity to design shoes. And Nike was getting a good deal because they were getting a Color Designer along with a Footwear Designer 1. Renee could do both jobs for one low price. This made financial sense since Exeter was only created to house their value channel brands. Instead of Renee continuing to design shoes off the books which could have brought with it legal implications, he was made to feel that they were moving him forward. Exeter was a near perfect fit, and after two years Renee would finally be free from the one thing that he felt was holding him back; his lack of a design degree.

Most footwear design jobs will take 2 years of experience in lieu of a degree so taking on the extra responsibility was going to be worth it. He was determined to prove his worth as a Footwear Designer 1 so his upward mobility would finally increase. He could get off the bottom rung and hopefully propel our family into a better financial situation. If he did well in this position he could then work towards being promoted to a Footwear Design 2 position which had a starting salary of about 80,000 dollars per year. If he could secure that promotion I would be able to go back to school so I could get a better job and we could eventually look forward to a future without a boot on our neck.

At the time I was working as a caregiver at Benchview Place with my mom and sister but taking care of old people is hard work and low pay. Changing diapers, lifting people, watching people die. It wasn't easy working weekends at Benchview and then coming home to 4 small children. And it certainly wasn't easy for Renee to work all week and then be saddled with the kids all weekend while I worked but we did what we had to do to get by. Buying my childhood home hadn't exactly been a very informed decision. Fixing up the house required a lot of time and money that was in short supply. There wasn't a lot of time to come up for air.

When Renee went back to work the following day I was really

worried that Randy was going to try something again. "Mark my words" I had told him emphatically that evening "Randy isn't done." Renee had described a pattern to me that was disturbing and I was positive that Randy wasn't going to leave him alone. Randy had some kind of problem. I was very apprehensive about the whole thing. Renee had insisted to Haley and me that he had taken care of it. He didn't want to rock the boat unnecessarily. He was positive that after telling Randy to leave him alone that Randy would not try to touch him again.

But as the day drew to a close and Renee was leaving work Randy was back at it again. I was actually on the phone with him asking him how everything was going when his voice stiffened up "Honey hold on." I couldn't hear any talking just some muffled sounds and then "Fucking Randy." Renee was screaming in my ear and then silence. I was SCARED to death and I tried calling him back but there was nothing. His phone would ring and ring and ring.

I was so worried I could hear my heart beating in my chest. What just happened? Did Renee and Randy finally get into a physical fight? The clock went tick, tick, tick just as slow as it could. Qayden and Kamaya were fighting about something. Our little miniature dachshund Kapukei was whining to go outside. I started picking up the house to take my mind off the time. Where was he?

When Renee finally pulled up to the house I was relieved to see him and I ran outside to ask what happened. He was mad and it takes a lot to get Renee mad. Randy had groped him in the hallway. Randy had actually had the nerve to reach out and caress Renee's butt. Renee had pushed his hand away and said "No" but Randy had just smirked back at him putting his hands out to his sides as if to say "What" like what he was doing was just cute and innocent. Renee had glared back at him and Randy stuck his hand out asking for a low high five as if to say "are we cool?" And Renee had slapped it to end the interchange but things didn't feel cool. The minute he walked out the door he had screamed out his frustration just as his phone went dead. He didn't need to be dealing with this kind of shit at work.

I was relieved he was okay but he had scared me this time and I didn't need to be worried about this along with everything else we had going on. I kept insisting that he tell someone right away. Couldn't Nike just move him away from Randy? But Renee seemed so unsure about saying anything to anybody. It was just a fucked up situation all the way around.

Obviously the things that had happened were humiliating and not something he wanted to tell anybody about, but if Randy kept this type of behavior up there was bound to be a physical altercation, and that wasn't going to end well. I kept forcefully insisting that he should complain. This was not okay. Someone had to put a stop to this crap. I had warned him that Randy wasn't going to leave him alone and I had been right. He finally agreed to tell somebody what was going on.

THE COMPLAINT

On March 5th 2007 my husband complained to his manager Richard "Mac" McDevitt. He wrote up a statement of what had happened so he wouldn't find himself at a loss for words and read it aloud to Mac who immediately contacted Mary Brunke from Human Resources and what a Mistake that turned out to be. I use the word "Mistake" with a capital M because what happened after my husband complained was not anything that we could have ever imagined.

At first Mac had seemed genuinely concerned. But Mary's first reaction of rude nervous laughter was more telling of the company response we could expect. It was like she couldn't handle what Renee had just said and was looking for a way to break the silence. It was very immature. Mac gave her a stern look and she managed to compose herself. Mary contacted Melissa Marks who was the HR Director for Nike and together the two women performed a shallow 3 day investigation which entailed briefly interviewing Randy, Cory, and Renee.

They quickly closed the case on March 7th forcing my husband back to work with the very person he had complained about. He was shocked when Mary Brunke called him into a meeting and handed him a closure letter that was unsigned and misleading of the allegations. She very flippantly informed him that they had corrected the behavior but she would not say how. She told him that the company had determined from their investigation that what Randy had done was just "roughhousing" and that Randy "had no idea" that he had offended anyone. My husband just sat across from her feeling stunned. He politely asked "Are they going move me?" Mary seemed taken aback.

Well Renee asked "Are they going to move Randy." Mary became indignant and looked surprised like why in the world would they be moving Randy? She said the word "No" looking at Renee like he had completely lost his mind. It was like he had no right to even ask that question. He was absolutely stunned. Mary waited for a few moments in Renee's stunned silence and then pushed some pamphlets towards him urging him to seek counseling if he felt he needed it.

The closure letter she handed him stated that Renee should enjoy a pleasant and professional working relationship with Randy. It was like what? Are you joking me right now? I couldn't believe my eyes when he showed me the letter later that night. How could they even make that suggestion? He had called me from work that day sounding tired and stressed so I knew something had gone terribly wrong but I couldn't have imagined that this would be it. It was not the outcome we had expected.

So we know Nike didn't get it but I know that all of you out there who have regular lives hear what I am saying? What? Who wants to deal with that kind of shit at work? And more importantly why? Why should someone have to deal with that kind of shit at work? It's not like Nike was a public place where Renee could have knocked Randy out if he had wanted to. This was the Nike campus and if something happened it would be Renee's word against Randy's.

Randy was older, white and well established with the company and Renee wasn't. If the police were called who do you think they were going to haul off? We didn't have time or energy for all this. Renee wasn't in the mood to be manhandled at work. Life was already stressful enough. Why couldn't they just move him? What was it to Nike to just move him somewhere? He emailed Human Resources reiterating that he no longer felt safe or comfortable around Randy but nobody seemed to care.

And after complaining Renee was determined to be moved away from Randy or to have Randy moved away from him. First of all it was very uncomfortable because it was like the whole office knew. Exeter was a small place and either the walls could talk or Mac, Mary,

Melissa, Cory, and Randy couldn't keep their mouths shut. Renee had to get out of there. It was a reasonable request. He was only making about 60,000 dollars per year so he wasn't some high paid employee that was asking to be catered to. Things between him and Cory were weird enough but having to continue seeing Randy everyday was just way too much!

Randy's office nickname "Big Daddy" had suddenly taken on a sinister meaning. Renee had never really been comfortable with the name in the first place but in the beginning he had settled on calling Randy "Bigs" just to be polite. Everyone at the office called Randy "Big Daddy" even Clare Hamill who had recently replaced Lisa Kempa as president and CEO of Exeter referred to Randy as "Big Daddy." Renee felt he had to try to fit in somehow. It was hard being the only person of color at Exeter and he had to pick and choose his battles. But now after everything that he had witnessed Randy was just plain old Randy and Renee kept his distance. Sometimes a person is just done. Randy had broken the last straw.

So after the investigation Renee was openly avoiding Randy which made the office environment especially stressful. He wasn't taking any chances. Despite what Mary had told him he just didn't trust Randy anymore. You can't force somebody to trust somebody. Trust is earned. We couldn't understand why they were refusing to move him. It seemed like a no brainer to us.

We've all been in situations where two people aren't getting along and you know how uncomfortable that can be? But this wasn't just a case of two people not getting along. This was a case of someone having done something so "OUT THERE" in terms of what we all consider normal workplace behavior and I don't care if you are gay or straight. Doesn't matter! Nobody needed to be touching anybody. I think we can all agree on that. That's something you are supposed to learn in Kindergarten. You know the rule "Keep your hands to yourself" It's not that hard.

I was of the opinion that if Randy wanted to do "All that" he could do "All that" somewhere else. Not in front of people or to people without their consent. I was very Very VERY upset! Renee had worked up at Nike for 8 years and he had never asked for anything. It was reasonable for him to not want to work with Randy anymore. It certainly would have made me feel better if they moved somebody, and it certainly would have made Renee feel better. In fact it would have probably made the whole office feel better. It had become painfully obvious that everybody thought they knew something. Suddenly there wasn't enough room on the entire Nike campus for Renee and Randy.

People started acting funny. Every interchange seemed more forced than the last. Renee just wanted out of there. He didn't care where they moved him. He didn't even care if they moved him or Randy. Have you seen Nike's World Headquarters? The place looks like Disneyland. Surely they could have easily diffused the situation by taking the small step of separating the two. How they dealt with Randy was their business but Renee just didn't want to work with the guy anymore. That was fair. So on March 12th 2007 he filed what we believed would be a cut and dry government complaint with The Equal Employment Opportunity Commission otherwise known as the EEOC. We figured since Randy had admitted to what he had done that the EEOC would just tell Nike to "Do the right thing" pun intended.

This was an emergency and we then took the time to drive up to the EEOC Seattle Field Office in hopes of speeding up the process. We were hoping for a quick resolution. Certainly the EEOC should be able to nudge Nike in the right direction. On arrival to the office we were greeted by a pleasantly plump African American secretary who made us watch a video about the charge process. The video made it very clear that filing a charge did not mean you would get any "Money." She then led us back to a drab little office where we waited to speak to an investigator who would determine if our situation warranted filing a charge of discrimination. The video had explained that we would only be allowed to file a charge if the investigator thought that the situation we presented warranted an action like that.

So Matthew Cleman appeared moments later looking tired and like he would rather be somewhere else. He was thin with brown hair and big bushy eyebrows. His clothes were disheveled and wrinkled as if he had slept in them the night before and he seemed genuinely surprised when Renee handed him the closure letter that he had received. "They gave you this?" He questioned Renee with a surprised tone in his voice. Obviously the story Renee had just told coupled with the letter he was staring at meant something really did happen.

From the expression on his face it appeared that this was the most excitement he had had in a long time. Suddenly he became more animated and left the room to take a copy of the letter. When he returned he explained more about the process. He seemed confident that this was a matter for the EEOC and he helped Renee draft a charge of sexual harassment and sex discrimination. It was our belief that if Renee had been a woman they would have moved him away from Randy right away. Matthew explained that Nike would officially receive the charge in 7 to 10 business days and then the EEOC would begin their investigation.

At the time we thought the whole thing would be over rather quickly. Renee's only request at the time was that he not have to work with Randy anymore. Matthew assured us that the company could not retaliate against Renee for filing the complaint. He said that as long as he had an open charge pending that Nike could not do anything to change his position at the company. He said that was the law.

He reassured us that if Nike fired him or demoted him or did anything, then that would be considered retaliation which was against the law. That was certainly a big concern for both of us considering the company's initial reaction. But we really hoped it wasn't like that. Surely once Nike got the EEOC complaint they would take the matter seriously and just move somebody. Renee didn't want to get anybody in trouble he just wanted things to go back to some kind of normal. But on March 20th 2007 before we had gotten anything figured out there was more bad news.

A DEATH IN THE FAMILY

I remember that morning. For some reason I think I was going to drop him off at Nike because I was in the car in the driver's seat waiting for him. He came out the front door and his cell phone started to ring. He stopped to answer the call and then he called out to me "My dad is dead." I was trying to process what he said when his knees buckled and he grabbed our porch railing in an effort to stop his own fall. He looked like he was going to faint. I jumped out of the car and rushed over to help him. He kept asking me what he should do. I guided him back inside the house and told him to sit down. I gave him a Lorazepam to calm his nerves while he continued to get the full story from his brother. The nerve racking situation at his work already had me so on edge that I had gone to the doctor a few days ago and gotten a little something to help with my growing anxiety.

Every day when Renee was at work I was worrying myself sick frightened that Randy was going to do something again. I didn't like the idea of Renee still working with Randy and I was really hoping for a swift response from the EEOC so we could be done with that situation. And now this? This was bad. This was really really bad. No preschool for Kamaya and Qayden today. I clicked on the television and popped in "The Gods Must be Crazy" to occupy the kids. That along with "ET" were the only movies as of late guaranteed to keep the kids quiet for a couple of hours. I opened the pill bottle and swallowed my own dose of Lorazepam. I needed to calm down as well.

The death of Renee's dad presented us with yet another difficult predicament. Things had always been tense between his family and me so they had never really liked me. It had a lot to do with the way we first met. It also might have had something to do with my loud opinionated ways but the women in Renee's family were loud and opinionated to. They had made it pretty clear from day one that I would never be accepted. Of course the way we had gotten together hadn't helped my introduction to the family. I had asked Renee to take me to my senior prom when he was still just a junior in high school. It would be our very first date.

We were both attending Jefferson High School at the time. He had borrowed his brother's Cadillac to take me to a wonderful dinner of filet mignon down at the Benson Hotel where to his horror he had watched me take just 3 or 4 bites of the 40 dollar a plate meal. Those were the good "ole" days and there wasn't a lot of room in my size 3 dress that evening. I had noticed him having some trouble maneuvering the car when we left the house that night and I had offered to drive my little car but he said he could handle it. Now here we were careening off the road and my life was flashing before my eyes.

We were following my friend Amanda and her boyfriend Eugene to the venue. It was pouring down rain and when Eugene made a sudden lane change Renee had tried to follow but the Cadillac was big and clunky and the tires were bald. He lost control of the car and instead of taking the exit we ended up hitting a light pole. We had been going about 50 miles per hour on the freeway and there was a big tree standing just inches from the light pole. If we had hit that tree we would have both been killed and this story would be over but we must have had a guardian angel watching over us that night. The light pole gave so instead of the engine ending up in our laps which would have been the case if we had hit the tree the engine was instead crumpled up close to the front window.

We were both wearing our seat belts and we were alive. Only one curl from my JC Penney hairdo had fallen out of place. That was some kind of bionic hairspray! My chest kind of hurt from the impact from the seatbelt but thankfully we were both in one piece.

When Renee saw the damage to his brother's car he literally tried to walk out into oncoming traffic. I must admit it didn't look good.

I called out to him and grabbed his arm and he turned back to me and hugged me so hard it hurt. He was crying and I was trying to tell him it would be okay. Amanda and Eugene had seen our car fly off the road and they came back for us. After the police took a statement we jumped into the backseat of Eugene's car in hopes of still making an appearance at the prom. We arrived in time enough to take a picture and dance to Blackstreet's "Before I let you go." Then the prom was over and Amanda and Eugene drove us both home.

When we dropped Renee off we all offered to come inside to help explain what happened but he told us not to. I didn't know Renee very well at that time. We had had few classes together. I had asked him to prom because at the time I had no one to go with and he had always seemed like a really nice intelligent guy and I was desperate. He was kind of quiet but when he spoke he would usually ask the most intriguing questions. One time in math class when I dropped my pencil he retrieved it for me and our hands had touched briefly and I felt an intense energy. It was kind of scary but it also made me curious to get to know him better. It was like we had some kind of connection already.

When I got home that night my chest continued to hurt and I ended up in the Emergency Room diagnosed with a chest wall contusion from the accident. Renee's family was worried that I would want to put in a claim on their insurance. The Cadillac was uninsured so that presented a major problem for them. His sisters had already convinced themselves that I had been "doing something" in the car to make Renee crash. The women in the family were worried about a lawsuit. Renee's dad Roy was the only one to ask if I was okay and thankfully his older brother Michael was surprisingly understanding and forgiving.

But it was not a good decision to listen to Renee on the night of the accident. At least I should have gone into the house to introduce myself but hindsight is always 20/20. Opinions and attitudes were formed in my absence and first impressions tend to hold a lot of water. I was on the outs from day one. But Renee and I had become inseparable. Something had happened that night in the car. Something or someone had saved us and when he hugged me out there on the dark freeway I knew he was the one.

We began dating and within just a few weeks he had become a

permanent fixture in my life. Even though he hadn't quite finished his junior year of high school he moved into my room and we were living together. This didn't make his family very happy. He was the responsible son who had a bright future and I was looking like a big distraction.

At 16 he had acquired an internship at Adidas International through a joint venture with Self Enhancement to introduce inner city kids to the footwear industry. He was selected out of a group of participants to be a model shop assistant. Adidas was very happy with his work so when the internship ended they decided to keep him around. So at the time he was working at Adidas and going to Jefferson at the same time. He was kind, easy going, and well-liked by everyone. When Adidas began their Color Design unit he was given shoes to color by hand and as the Color Design industry grew Renee grew with it.

He was by my side at my graduation and just a few months later when he was still just 17 years old he proposed at the Spaghetti Factory in front of my entire family. I can't remember the speech he made that night but the whole restaurant was clapping when I said yes. We must have looked more than a little silly though. We were very young to be having such a whirlwind romance and we looked it. The following year he was still attending Jefferson High School as a senior and I would drop him off and pick him up when I could.

I had decided to go to Portland Community College instead of making my mother try to pay for a more expensive school. She really wanted me to go to a nice liberal arts college like my sister's had but I just wasn't feeling it. I had seen the stress she had endured putting my two sisters and one of my brothers through college and I wasn't interested in being a part of that. I didn't even really believe she could do it anyway. We had already lived without heat for 3 years and I didn't want to further contribute to my mother's financial problems. Plus I just wasn't sure if college was for me. I was going to make my own way and I secretly dreaded being away from Renee for any real period of time. Once he graduated from high school we planned to get our own place. Staying in Portland felt right at the time.

Over the years Renee and I would visit his family often to try to build a relationship but it was hard. Renee's dad made the situation easier because at least he was always glad to see us. Roy always had an infectious smile, a kind word, and an interesting story to tell. He met Angie while visiting the Philippines on tour with the military. They were quickly married and in a few short months when she was 9 months pregnant with Renee's brother Michael, Angie made her way to the United States in hopes of a better life.

But unfortunately Roy's career in the military was short lived. He was honorably discharged after just 6 months. He became a security guard and the growing family struggled to make ends meet. They ended up in the projects of San Francisco and with both parents working all of the time the 4 kids formed a close bond. The neighborhood wasn't safe and they spent a lot of time watching television dreaming of a better life.

Angie was a survivor and she quickly resigned herself to the cold harsh reality of her new life. She had discovered like a lot of immigrants that the American Dream was really just a dream. She worked hard to raise her kids and hoped like most parents that they would do better than her and Roy had. When Roy received a 20,000 dollar settlement from a wrist injury on the job the family struck out from California to Oregon in search of a better life.

The move was hard on the kids and they dropped out of school one by one. First Michael so he could get a job to buy the things he needed and wanted. Then Toinette who got pregnant at just 15 years old and finally Michelle who had fallen behind her peers without notice in the broken educational system. The kids had a hard life and they didn't see how going to school was going to make it any better. They felt inadequate without the right clothes, shoes, and social status. Renee just kept going to school to make his mother proud. He wanted so much for his mother to be happy but despite how hard Roy and Angie worked the family was constantly on welfare and life could be very depressing at times.

On July 25th 1998 Renee and I were officially married at The Wedding House. I was already 8 months pregnant with Qadira when my brother Uranus walked me down the aisle. Most of our guests were Renee's friends from Adidas where he was still working at the time. His mother sang "Little things mean a lot" entertaining the crowd with her beautiful singing voice. She had once dreamed of being a famous singer but that was not the life she got so for now this would have to do. At least we all managed to get along that day. It was a happy day for everybody. Despite all of our past differences, on that day the future looked very bright.

We had hoped that after the wedding his family would be more accepting of our relationship but some things never change. The day came and went and my status with the family never changed. It put a constant strain on our marriage but we endured. In 1999 after hitting the glass ceiling at Adidas Renee had with the help of an old friend made the move to Nike. Now instead of a mere 30,000 a year he was making 45,000 a year. We needed it.

The kids were set to come quickly, first Qadira in 1998, then Kymani in 2000, Kamaya in 2003 and finally Qayden in 2004. Our running joke is that once we figured out where they were coming from Renee went and got that fixed. The truth was we couldn't afford anymore at the time even if we had wanted more. Renee's climb up the corporate ladder at Nike was slow going. And when Qayden arrived shortly after we purchased the house our plate was very full.

We worked hard at having a relationship with his family despite our contentious relationship. We tried to bring the kids to visit them at least once a week because they rarely made it a priority to visit us. My parents were divorced and I had never been close to my dad who drowned in 2002. Roy was the only Grandfather that our children had. And while it is true that Angie couldn't bring herself to accept me she genuinely loved her grandchildren. I didn't want to be responsible for getting in the way of that. We learned for the most part to tolerate one another. Sometimes we even got along just fine. But it was hard.

This was Renee's family and for better or worse they were mine and we all had to find a way to cope with one another. Renee and I encountered a lot of frustration and misunderstandings along the way and there were definitely times when we considered ending our marriage over it. Sometimes it was just so painful. It can really suck to be married into a family that doesn't accept you and sometimes I would get so mad and take it out on him. It wasn't fair that my family accepted Renee but his family didn't accept me. It was the cause of many arguments over the years. But Renee really loved his family and Renee really loved me. We made it work because there was no other way.

As the year 2006 drew to a close Renee's parents along with his sisters and brother decided to move back to California. Roy hadn't been in the best health when they decided to make the move and he had always said that he wanted to die in California but nobody could have guessed that it would happen so soon. Now just 3 months after getting settled back in California Michael was calling to deliver the bad news. Roy had suffered for years with Type 2 Diabetes and Congestive heart failure and we knew he wasn't in the best of health but he was only 63 when he passed. We were shocked. And to make matters worse our last visit had ended in a terrible screaming match and Renee had for the very first time asked his entire family to leave our house.

This unfortunate family drama which had occurred in January of 2007 just before they struck out for California had now made a painful situation even worse. Renee hadn't got a chance to speak with his father before he died and now he was going to have to live with that. He had had so much going on at work and they had moved so far away. It was a lot to be dealing with especially with an 8, 6, 4, and 2 year old in tow. Now we were packing up the kids and heading to Sacramento for a funeral.

When we arrived Renee was already so devastated and Michael, Michelle, and Toinette didn't help the situation by insisting that I be left out of the obituary because "I wasn't really family." It's not like we were expecting a good time but we thought at least people would try to be cordial. Isn't there always some kind of drama even when the closest of families get together? Well our kind of family drama was 10,000 times worse.

We even had to go to separate viewings. The memory of the last argument hung heavy in the air and there was certainly enough blame to go around and most of it was being thrown directly at me. After the funeral service Renee's mom invited us over for dinner and we all managed to get along long enough to have at least a short visit. But it was Renee's dad who had connected us. He was the one who had accepted me and now he was gone. After Roy died Renee mostly stopped hearing from his family.

We returned home after a very stressful two weeks apprehensive with still no word from the EEOC. When Renee went back to work his manager asked him to start taking direction from a new guy named Shawn Wenzel but nobody said anything about his complaint. We didn't know what to think. At this point Nike had definitely received the charge. It was nerve racking to say the least.

Shawn was mostly focused on the NASCAR Promo business but working with Shawn didn't mean that Renee was mostly focused on the NASCAR business it just meant that Renee didn't have to take direction from Randy anymore. It was a small concession considering that Renee was still working in close proximity to Randy and Cory and they still shared a workload as Exeter designers.

The change just meant that Renee wouldn't have to go directly to Randy for direction if he had any questions or needed any help. But the tension in the air was so thick it covered the office like a thick coat of polar bear fur. It was like a poisonous bomb had gone off in the office. People made it clear whose side they were on. It was a unified front. Exeter was small and it was perfectly clear that it was Renee who was no longer welcome.

Randy was a big time designer who had designed one of the first pairs of Tiger Woods shoes. He was making something like 150,000 dollars a year and he did what he wanted. He was certainly more valuable than Renee. I mean the guy could insist on being called "Big Daddy" on the job and people complied. Cory was also a senior designer making more or as much as Randy. He was also clearly more valuable than Renee and he knew how to keep his mouth shut.

We found out much later that Cory had claimed in the initial investigation that he remembered nothing of Randy's actions towards him which should have been a major red flag. At the time he was just more concerned that Skip Lei and another co-worker named Jen were having a very exclusive relationship that was causing him to feel uncomfortable at the office. But that bit of information was also disregarded. Nobody cared about Cory or his feelings or anything that he had to say. It was Renee that they were focused on. It was Renee who was the problem.

How dare he bring any of this up and cause the company so much trouble. Nobody wanted to be dealing with this and Renee was going to pay dearly for what he had done. The corporate hazing of my husband had begun the minute he opened his mouth to complain. After all who in the hell was Renee to say anything about anything that Randy had done? He was just a lowly pee on. Randy was so obviously more valuable than Renee that just the very fact that Renee had had the nerve to open his mouth meant that he must be taught a lesson. It was a terribly stressful time and we were hardly prepared for what happened just days after returning from Roy's funeral.

THE BURN

It was my youngest daughter Kamaya who knew something was terribly wrong on the night of April 12th 2007. At 4 years old she had sensed something and she awoke from a deep sleep screaming and crying for her sister. "Qadira" she yelled "Qadira" her voice was filled with panic. I ran up to her room where she was already on her way out the door with tears streaming down her already puffy cheeks. "Mom" she screamed at me "Mom you have to call Qadira." She was hysterical and I tried to calm her down. I tried to explain to her that Qadira was having an overnight and that she was fine but she just shook her head full of curls defiantly insisting that something was wrong. "Mom" she sobbed "PLEASE!" she was positively frantic at this point.

I thought I would just pick up the phone and call Qadira so Kamaya could speak to her and see that she was okay but that's not what happened. On that night I found my 8 year old daughter naked on a couch in a dark basement with her left leg all burned up and I didn't know what to do. She was just supposed to be having an overnight with a friend to help take her mind off things after going to the funeral. She had been excited to go. But now she was naked and injured and I had no idea what I had just walked into.

My neighbors Todd Burkholder and Aimee McQuiston were part of that older, white, well established group that my neighborhood was filled with. They were a little grungier than the regular crowd and I didn't see that Aimee was super tight with any of the mom's at the school. You know how moms have their groups? Well I didn't

31

see that she was in one. Kind of like me. I was still learning this new neighborhood and I was actively trying to reserve judgment when it came to my neighbor's. I wanted to fit into the neighborhood but I still was having trouble understanding the new crowd. We had made sort of a huge commitment to live in this neighborhood when we bought the house. Even if we could eventually sell it was going to be a while before we would be going anywhere. I was trying to do my best to make new friends and be social.

Todd and Aimee lived just two blocks away. Their daughter Sophie was an outspoken chubby little white girl with blond hair that had latched onto Qadira in Kindergarten just a few months after we moved into the neighborhood. She could be a little irritating sometimes calling our house 6, 7, 8 times a night usually in the middle of dinner. Sophie was obviously used to getting her way. Her father Todd appeared professional but was grungy and overly talkative. He was your typical Birkenstock wearing granola eating over privileged hippie that you cannot avoid in a city like Portland. He was one of those kinds of people who liked to stand too close and his words usually ran away with his mouth.

Talk, talk, talk, talk, talk, and talk as if you needed his full opinion on everything. I didn't really know what to make of the guy but whatever. He was just the father of my daughter's friend so I only had to put up with him now and again. He especially liked to brag about how smart his daughter was constantly pointing out to whoever would listen how bright little Sophie was. It got to be pretty irritating after a while but what can you do? I frequently felt uncomfortable around him because he always seemed to be invading my space but I never said anything. My strategy was always to be polite and terminate the conversation as quickly as possible.

The truth was I was uncomfortable around a lot of my neighbors. Just like when I was a kid, it wasn't easy being one of the only people of color in my neighborhood. I was a fish out of water and very unsure of myself in those days. Renee and I had done our share of moving around as we had the kids. We lived in outer SE Portland, Aloha, Tigard, but SW Portland was just a whole new ball game. All of the neighborhood's we lived in before were at least full of people our age at our socioeconomic level. Sure some were above and some below but we fit the general average. Our kids had what their friends had, maybe a little more or maybe a little less. These people always had way more and there kids always had way more. When we lived in a level playing field it was easier to know how to navigate social situations. I was a little lost here. I was suddenly being made to rub shoulders with a whole different class of people then what I was used to.

Todd's wife Aimee was a mousy brown haired overweight woman. She never looked happy or sad. Just sort of like a robot going through the mom motions. Not like Todd and Sophie who pranced around confidently all of the time. She seemed a little unsure of herself. But she was always cordial and we would make small talk. She wasn't really someone I could imagine myself being friends with but I tried to get to know her a little bit because Qadira was spending so much time hanging out with Sophie at school.

Eventually things progressed and Qadira and Sophie started having the occasional "play date." No more just going out and meeting up with friends in the street like in our old neighborhood in Aloha. Kids in SW Portland had "play dates." The concept wasn't completely foreign to me. Qadira had had a wealthy friend in preschool who had invited her to a few "play-dates." But this was the norm in this neighborhood and it was going to take some getting used to.

So Qadira and Sophie would have play-dates' and sometimes when we picked her up or they picked up Sophie we would stop and chat making little efforts along the way to try to get to know Todd and Aimee. Again I wasn't sure what to make of Aimee. She was just kind of around. She certainly wasn't animated like Todd. She was just sort of quiet and she was Sophie's mom and so she was someone I now had to deal with every now and again. How well can you really get to know all of your kid's friends' parents? It's not like I had a bunch of extra hours in the day to be socializing. I did invite her out to dinner and karaoke once to try to get to know her even a little better and she confided in me that Todd had had an affair. We didn't know each other well enough for me to have an opinion on that situation. And I wasn't about to try to get his side of the story. I was certainly old enough to be aware that most marriages have their pitfalls, but not confident enough to be giving marriage advice to someone who had a few years on me and that I didn't know very well. I needed to keep my mouth shut and my nose clean if I wanted to "make it" in this neighborhood. I wasn't about to start reading things into a one-time conversation and running my mouth about stuff I knew nothing about.

At this time Renee and I had kind of established a "no overnight" rule but Sophie began to persist in asking over and over if Qadira could spend the night. Todd had even questioned us at length about our reasons for not letting Qadira stay the night on one occasion after there had been a school function at the park. But when this all started up the girls were only in the first grade and we didn't know their family very well. It was just outside of our comfort zone and we told them that. But Sophie began to beg incessantly for Qadira to stay the night. It seemed to have become a little obsession of hers.

She would call the house to ask about it again and again and again. And eventually we relented allowing Qadira to stay the night for a birthday party with a group of girls and then a while later on her own because we had let her stay over before. We even had Sophie spend the night at our house one time and it didn't seem like too big of a deal. Renee never really was comfortable with these overnights but I had let my own feelings of inferiority dictate my decisions about how to handle our new neighbors. I was trying hard to fit in.

I encouraged Renee to give our neighbors the benefit of the doubt. It seemed harmless enough at the time. We were so busy with kids and work it was so hard to pay attention to the signs much less interpret them. So when Renee had a bad feeling about letting Qadira spend the night at Sophie's on April 12th 2007 he brushed it aside letting Qadira go anyway. It was this decision that has continued to haunt him to this day.

Aimee's voice had sounded calm that night when I called to ask to let Kamaya speak to Qadira. "Did I get her message?" She asked. "Qadira got a burn" she said breathlessly. What? A burn? I didn't understand what she was saying. I thought to myself. She must mean like a little burn on her finger. Like the kind you get when you are baking cookies? It couldn't be too big of a deal because Qadira wasn't usually the type of kid to get upset over those types of things. "Do I need to come?" I asked and she replied "Yes." I was a little perplexed because I couldn't really imagine Qadira wanting me to come look at some tiny little burn on her finger. That didn't seem like her but they only lived a couple blocks away so I could just pop over there, kiss the "booboo" and make it all better and be home in less than 10 minutes.

JUSTICE FOR QADIRA

When I got to their house Aimee met me at the door. Her face was flushed and red and she told me to come quickly leading me down the hallway down the stairs into their basement. Where was she taking me I wondered? Why was Aimee taking me to the basement? But when I got partway down the stairs I could see Qadira wrapped in a towel on the couch. Why was she wrapped in a towel? Sophie was off to the side and Lilo and Stitch was playing on the television. When Qadira saw me she immediately burst into tears. Her face was already so swollen and I raced to her side to soothe her. "Mommy I got a burn she cried."

I pulled back the towel and she was naked. What? But why was she naked? I couldn't understand what was happening but I knew my daughter was injured. Todd was shaking a dirty tube of aloe vera at me exclaiming "I was just gonna put some aloe vera on it." I pushed his hand away and removed the slightly warm bag of peas that was covering my daughter's thigh. I couldn't even begin to comprehend what I was looking at. Her skin looked wet where the bag had sat and it took me a moment to realize that I wasn't looking at her skin. I was staring at her open flesh. Aimee was saying something faintly in the background about the girls playing in the bathtub and Qadira standing on the edge and slipping in and that she had burned Qadira with a tea kettle.

Why had the kids been taking a bath? Why was there a teakettle in the bathroom? Weren't they supposed to be playing with Sophie's new kitten? What was going on? I didn't know these people well enough for it to be okay for our children to bathe together. Besides the girls were 8 years old! WHAT THE FUCK WAS GOING ON!? Oh my God what was happening? I looked over at Aimee whose cheeks had now grown a dark purple color. They were too old to be taking a bath together. Why were they taking a bath? Why was my daughter naked? What was happening? But I didn't have time to figure out what was going on. I could hear my heart pounding. First things first Qadira was hurt and she needed some help. Todd kept rambling on and I wished he would shut the hell up. I needed some time to think. But there was no time for that.

Everything was all wrong. I had to get out of there. I picked up Qadira and walked towards the basement stairs. They both started to follow me. Todd was asking me if I wanted to take the peas but I told him we had food at home. Why was this man trying to give me

35

a bag of peas? Aimee and Todd were rushing up the stairs behind me insisting that Qadira didn't need to go to the hospital but I kept telling them that I would take her anyway.

As I left I remember blurting out "Accidents happen; I have insurance." I wanted to get away from them. But when I got in the car I felt unsure of myself. Maybe I was overreacting? Maybe they were right; maybe I just needed to put some aloe vera on it. I didn't know what to think. Todd and Aimee had seemed so calm. How come they didn't seem to think that Qadira needed to go to the hospital? I decided to go home first and see what Renee thought about the situation.

I didn't want to make any unnecessary trips to the Emergency Room. That could mean 4 or 5 hours at the hospital. My oldest sister always made fun of me referring to me as a "mother bear." Renee's family and most of my aunt's had made me feel silly for nursing each child for about a year. They would say I "ruined" the babies because all of my kids when they were babies had wanted to be held all the time by me or Renee. They didn't like to be held by just anybody. Most of them would go to my mom for a while because she visited them frequently but even her magic touch tended to wear off after a while. Maybe I was overreacting? I decided to head home and get Renee's opinion before racing off into the night.

I couldn't think as I walked up my porch stairs. I had Qadira cradled in my arms wrapped in the towel I had found her in. When I got inside I called out to Renee to come. When your child is hurt you don't want it to be serious and I just wanted Qadira to be okay. I wanted Renee to tell me that she was going to be okay. But when he walked into the room he just stared. He just stood there staring. Renee couldn't help shed any light on the situation.

I laid Qadira on the sofa and he just kept staring down at her leg with a confused look on his face. Finally he asked me "What is that?" I tried to explain but it was like he couldn't hear me or I wasn't saying the right things. At the present moment I was saying something about a bathtub and a teakettle and a bag of peas that I could barely understand. He just kept standing there speechless. He wasn't helping me assess the situation at all and Qadira didn't look well. So I did what any kid would do, I called my mom. My mom would know what to do.

I grabbed the phone and dialed up her number as fast as I could.

It was ringing, ringing, and click. "Hello." All my mom remembers is me screaming into the phone. "Mom!" I started sobbing relieved to hear her voice. "Mom Qadira got a burn!" I screamed. "Her leg is all burned up" Suddenly I was crying so hard I could barely talk.

I was gasping for air. But my mom was calm "Okay." She said "Is there any skin on her leg?" She asked. "No" I replied staring down at Qadira's open flesh trying to understand what I was looking at. "Take her to the hospital right now." My mother's voice was firm and it pierced through the fog that had enveloped me. I needed to go to the hospital right now. Finally somebody knew what to do.

The seconds ticked by like hours. As I hung up the phone I realized that we needed someone to watch the kids. Renee and I felt scared and worried and Qadira looked miserable. Her eyes were practically glued shut from crying. I called my mom back and she said she would come right away but now it seemed like she was taking forever.

We obviously were not thinking clearly because we decided to call Todd and Aimee and ask them to come over and watch our other kids so we could leave right away. Shock is real and it can cloud your judgment immensely. I know it sounds bizarre us calling the very people who had just harmed our daughter to come watch our other kids but that is exactly what we did.

Qadira was looking pale and shaky. But we had just put our 3 youngest kids in bed and we couldn't leave them alone. I didn't feel comfortable just knocking on anyone's door. It was late. What if we were wrong? What if Qadira wasn't that hurt and we were just going to be waking up our neighbor's for no reason? I didn't really know anybody in the neighborhood well enough to go bothering them with this. But on the other hand everything seemed incredibly urgent. There was no skin on Qadira's leg. Someone had poured SCALDING water on her. We needed to get her checked out right away and I wanted Renee to sit with Qadira in the back seat of the car because I wouldn't be able to belt her and someone needed to be watching her to make sure she was okay.

Todd arrived alone and we were a bit taken aback. He sauntered in looking relaxed and proclaimed loudly that we were overreacting "If it was my daughter I would just put some Aloe Vera on it" He bellowed. I felt a flash of anger as we walked out the door. We needed to get out of there. I didn't have time to regret calling him or to wonder where Aimee was. We loaded Qadira into the car and left in a hurry. I told Todd that as soon as my mom arrived he could leave and I meant it. He was irritating me and I didn't want him in my house. I just wanted someone to tell me that my daughter was going to be okay. I decided to go to what I believed was the nearest hospital. Which was closer Legacy Emanuel or Providence St Vincent's? Providence seemed closer so I headed in that direction. And so it was on April 12th 2007 not long after I discovered Qadira all burnt up in our neighbor's basement we arrived at Providence Saint Vincent's Hospital in search of help for our daughter.

It had been about a half an hour since Aimee had led me down into the basement. Everything was a blur. I was led to a chair for check in. Renee had disappeared with Qadira. They had wheeled her straight back and he had gone with her. The admitting nurse was asking me what happened and I told her what I knew which wasn't much at the time. She asked me. "Do you think this was abuse?" My heart started pounding. What was this lady talking about? What the FUCK? Where was my daughter? My daughter hadn't been abused. Why was she saying these things to me? I was frantic. My daughter was going to be fine. My heart was pounding so hard I could feel it beating in my ears. I firmly told her that I had no idea what those people had been doing. Why was she asking me what I thought? Where was my daughter? I wanted to see my daughter. Was she okay? Why was I sitting out here in the lobby when Qadira needed me?

Finally after what felt like an eternity she took me to see Qadira. She was laying on an emergency bed her face all puffed up and red from crying. Why hadn't they treated her yet? I was trying to comfort her when the same nurse who had been at the admitting desk came in with a big vile of Motrin, she shoved it into Qadira's mouth and instructed another male nurse to bandage her leg. Within minutes she was handing us some papers and sending us home.

The male nurse picked Qadira up and placed her in Renee's arms and directed us out the door. SLAP, KICK, PUNCH! What had felt like forever had actually only been 17 minutes. A little fact I wouldn't discover for years. That's right, you heard me, I said 17 FUCKING minutes! When does a visit to the emergency room ever take just 17 minutes? They didn't even put a blood pressure cuff on her. Just a few bandages and a smooth "get the fuck out" and we weren't even any the wiser. What did we know? We were trained to trust the authorities from a young age. After all why would the people in charge work together to lie to you?

We left the hospital and took Qadira home even though most of her tiny little leg was covered in bandages and she couldn't walk. She was diagnosed with a burn on 10-20% of her body. They gave us some discharge papers telling us to come back if things got any worse. Like things could really get any worse? So when we got up the next morning we had no idea what to do with Qadira. She was in terrible pain and we had no idea how to change her bandages or if we should change her bandages. We didn't even have any bandages. Renee had to go to work. He had already taken two weeks off for the funeral and he was afraid if he took more time off he might lose his job. How would he take care of all of this if he lost his job?

I was going to have to take Qadira back to the doctor by myself because obviously nothing was resolved. Renee called Todd and Aimee early that morning to get their Homeowners insurance in case they asked for it at Qadira's next visit. We all know how insurance works. Our insurance wasn't going to cover something that was somebody else's responsibility. Renee informed Aimee that Qadira's burns were bad and that he needed their insurance to make sure everything was covered. Aimee hemmed and hawed and told Renee she would call him back. Eventually Todd called back with the information but he still couldn't seem to understand why we were taking Qadira back to the doctor.

I took Qadira to Oregon Health Science University otherwise known as OHSU where she was seen by a Doctor Sarah Tubbesing. We had recently established care with the Gabriel Park OHSU Family Clinic and Qadira hadn't even met her new doctor yet. I had chosen Nancy Gorden-Zwerling because when I first met her she claimed that she knew and had worked with our kids' old pediatrician Mariah Taylor. You might know Mariah Taylor because she was on Oprah one time. She was the best doctor the kids ever had. She was warm and caring and you could just tell that she really loved children. We liked her so much that wherever we moved we would cart our kids out to North Portland to be seen by her at the small clinic where she worked servicing the poor and disadvantaged. But Mariah had retired and I wasn't going to make the drive to see just anybody working there.

Nancy Gorden-Zwerling wasn't available that day which is why we saw Sarah. She was a tall thin pretty young blond lady with a pleasant smile. But she looked just as confused as I felt when she took off Qadira's bandages. It was a MASSIVE wound and for some time Sarah just sat there and stared at it. The diagnosis from the Emergency Room doctor was a 2nd degree burn on 10 to 20 percent of her body. Sarah said she thought that maybe there were areas that were 3rd degree and she ran out of the room to grab a colleague to come look. Another doctor came into the room and behind her came several more. I didn't understand what was going on. Was Qadira okay? After a few minutes they all left and I was left all alone staring at my daughter's open wound.

Sarah came back after a while with some supplies and bandaged Qadira's leg back up. She calmly instructed me to go to the medical store and buy bandages and silvadene and to change Qadira's bandages 3 times a day. SLAP, KICK, PUNCH! She didn't show me how to change her bandages as if watching her that one time was supposed to be enough. She pretended like everything was fine even though Qadira couldn't walk and had a huge open wound on her leg. I was standing there in the office feeling a little stunned and unsure of what I was experiencing. So Qadira was fine?

Sarah kept smiling at me as if this was just a routine visit. She kept telling me over and over again that everything was going to be just fine. She reminded me again to go to the medical store and buy bandages and silvadene and further instructed me not to bring Qadira back to the hospital. I had now been told by a second doctor that my daughter was perfectly fine. Nobody even offered me the use of a wheelchair when I carried my daughter out of the clinic that day.

When I arrived home I was relieved that Qadira's bandages had been changed and I thanked my brother Uranus for watching the kids. For once I was really glad he was staying with us. Kymani, Kamaya, and Qayden still all needed looking after and I hadn't had time to get anybody to school that day. I called Renee at work and told him what they had said. We were just both so relieved that the doctor had told us that Qadira was going to be okay.

Renee said he knew where the medical store was and when he got home he would go buy the supplies and we could change Qadira's bandage together. I tucked Qadira safely away in our bed away from her brother and sister. I gave her some Tylenol with codeine the only prescription the doctor had prescribed and watched anxiously over her. She had to be carried back and forth to the bathroom and she was in a lot of pain but they had told us she was going to be okay. LET ME REPEAT SHOCK IS REAL! I had no idea that I was being lied to.

Two days into the bandage changes I had a bad feeling. The wound was red and weeping and I just felt that something was wrong. I called the number on the discharge papers and spoke to a doctor David Solondz. I told him that I thought Qadira's wound might be infected but he told me that I was doing everything right and he firmly instructed me not to come back to the hospital. This was the 3rd time I had been told by a medical professional that Qadira was fine so I resigned myself to the task at hand. My feelings must be wrong I told myself. It must be true that Qadira was fine even though she didn't look fine. But I still felt that something was wrong.

I decided to go ask my neighbor Alexander what he thought about the situation. Alexander had been a nurse in the military and maybe he could help. What if we weren't changing the bandages right? It's not like anyone had showed us how. I knew from my knowledge as a caregiver to use chucks pads and gloves but I still worried that we might be doing something wrong. Alexander came over and watched us do a bandage change. He said he thought we were doing a good job. Nobody ever asked us why Qadira wasn't in the hospital. Everyone around us had been well trained to never question authority. This was what the doctor's had told us to do and no one that encountered Qadira at that time questioned that. On April 16th I took Qadira back to OHSU to see a Doctor Randall Nacamuli. At this point I was absolutely convinced her leg was infected. He once again assured me everything was fine. After this visit we stopped trying to take Qadira back to the hospital.

The bandage changes were horrible. Her wound looked so HORRIFIC we were compelled to take pictures. We thought about calling the police but what could they do? They weren't going to help us change Qadira's bandages and we couldn't see anything beyond getting Qadira well. The doctors didn't tell us to call the police they told us that it was our job to take care of Qadira. We didn't have any reason to distrust the doctors. We had to listen to what the doctors had said and do as we were told if we wanted Qadira to get better.

The truth is people who are in shock are easy to boss around. They can't really think for themselves and at this point Renee and I had been through a lot. Each bandage change took about forty five minutes and Qadira would grit her teeth and cry as we fussed over her. She was just a tiny 59 pound 8 year old little girl and she had given up taking the Tylenol with codeine because she complained it made her feel "funny." She somehow endured the pain with just a little bit of plain Tylenol.

It was terrible to watch. Sometimes the bandages would get stuck to her open flesh and she would cry out in pain as we tried to carefully remove them and clean the open wound. It was HORRIFIC for everybody in the house but for her it must have felt like TORTURE. Little did we know that every time we had to change the bandage we were being further traumatized and we did this over and over and over and over again watching our little daughter grit her teeth and cry as we tried our best to help heal the gigantic burn on her leg. We had been told over and over by the authorities that is was OUR job to take care of Qadira.

Over the next two weeks we changed those bandages 3 to 6 times per day waiting for the skin to grow back. It took a tremendous amount of time, energy, and focus on our part. SLAP, KICK, PUNCH! We still had 3 other kids to care for on top of all this. We had to take the kids to school, go to work, and take care of Qadira. We hardly had a minute to sleep or eat. Kymani, Kamaya, and Qayden witnessed everything sometimes staying to comfort their sister through the process.

The kids struggled to hide their shock at the sight of her open flesh. My friend Amaya came by to visit and Qadira's little friend Sadira burst into tears when she saw Qadira all burned up laying on the bed. It was a shock to all who witnessed it. Amaya told me she didn't know if she could handle it if something like that happened to Sadira. But we were trying to be strong. Certainly we had been given no other choice. Someone had to take care of Qadira and falling apart was not an option. Things were not good but we needed to be brave for our daughter.

After about a week she was able to get around on some crutches but every time she moved the bandage would slip down below the knee and sometimes the wound would get dirty. The burn was located right over her left knee joint in a difficult to keep bandaged spot but we did the best we could do under the circumstances.

Qadira's teacher came by and paid her a visit acting like everything was totally normal. And soon after Todd called wanting to bring Sophie by with some get well cards from the kids at school. When they arrived we wondered where Aimee was and Sophie blurted out that her mom was grounded. What did Sophie mean? Why was Aimee grounded? Todd just talked and talked about everything. It was a weird visit. I felt uncomfortable around Todd. Why was he here? Where was Aimee? I didn't want these people in my house. It was the last time we really ever talked to them. Todd gave Qadira a card that read "We are so sorry you got hurt." SLAP, KICK, PUNCH! What the HELL was that even supposed to mean?

About this time our youngest daughter was also battling a case of pneumonia and I was struggling to care for both girls while Renee was at work. Kamaya had always been so sickly and it always seemed that she had some illness we were dealing with; a cold, flu, pneumonia. I had her enrolled in preschool but she had to be absent a lot. I tried to keep her home at the slightest hint of an illness because when she got sick it just seemed to wipe her out.

Nobody offered to help and I didn't even think to ask. Nobody even brought us a meal. And we had been very conditioned to always take care of everything by ourselves. Everybody in our lives was always busy with their own lives and we struggled along doing the best we could. It seems like a blur when I think back. Renee was afraid to take any more time off but he would come home when he could at lunchtime to help. The work situation was tense but we didn't have time to think about that. Thankfully the EEOC was going to take care of that.

Todd and Aimee had State Farm insurance and an agent called asking to come see about Qadira. Her name was Beth Phipps and she arrived at our door about two weeks after Qadira had been burned. SLAP, KICK, PUNCH! At this point I always felt kind of sick about everything. She insisted in a very official way on taking pictures of Qadira's wound which made me feel very very uncomfortable. I mean Qadira wasn't a car she was a child. It didn't feel right unwrapping Qadira's leg and allowing this woman to take pictures of her injury but she acted like she knew what she was doing. I mean once again I was just a high school graduate with 4 kids and this woman appeared to be someone in a position of authority. I watched her snap pictures of my daughters burned up leg. Her hands seemed a little shaky and she looked visibly ill for a moment after I unwrapped the wound which was looking a hell of a lot better than it had two weeks ago. She explained that the insurance company would probably offer some money but that they needed to see the extent of the damage to come to a decision. She also said that we would have to put the money in some kind of special account since Qadira was a child.

After Beth left I called Renee and told him what had happened. Something had felt wrong about the encounter and I thought maybe we should get an attorney. All the things Beth told me had been confusing and we weren't going to be wheeling and dealing with the insurance company over this. What did we know? It seemed to make sense to call someone who knew about these kinds of things. How could we possibly measure the impact that this experience would have on Qadira? How could we determine what a fair outcome would be? We were still busy dealing with the initial wound and knew nothing about any of that.

Renee called up Stephen P. Riedlinger of Susak & Powell. Steve had done a good job as Renee's attorney when he was in a car accident some years ago and Renee trusted him. Steve took the case on contingency right away which was nice. It was a relief because we didn't have the time or energy to deal with the insurance company and Qadira's injury at the same time. Renee was still grieving the loss of his dad and with no word from the EEOC things at work were getting tenser every day.

We did our best to care for Qadira and in about three weeks the burn had been replaced with mottled patchy looking skin. Her leg looked like it belonged to Frankenstein and at times she had trouble breathing. I took her to see Nancy Gorden-Zwerling where she was given an inhaler and referred to a Plastic surgeon. We took her to the plastic surgeon and he told us that Qadira was healing up just fine and that there was nothing he could do to make her leg look any better. That's just the way burns looked. But Qadira was so disfigured I just couldn't understand how everything was fine? He told me to make sure to keep the area covered with sunblock so it didn't get sunburned. I felt like someone had kicked me in the stomach.

This is what her leg was going to look like? All patchy and

mottled? From her lower thigh to down past her knee her leg looked like a patchwork quilt. It was like someone had taken several different legs and sewn them all together. Every time I saw it all I could think was that it looked like dead flesh. All of her shirts, shorts, and dresses were replaced with capris that kept the area covered at all times. Would her leg look this way forever? I found myself questioning God.

Why did Aimee have to burn Qadira? My heart was thudding loud in my ears. It sounded so loud I thought maybe the whole room could hear it. I managed a smile. Qadira was sitting there on the table and I needed to stay focused. I told the doctor "Okay." I made sure to keep my voice steady and calm. He said maybe when she was older she could get surgery but that the scarring would always be there. SLAP, KICK, PUNCH! It was a lot to take in. It shook me to my core. She was only 8 years old. She was just finishing second grade. All I could do was hope that things got better.

It was after this visit that I was contacted by Scott F Kocher of Vangelisti Kocher LLP. He called me up one day and said that he was a special burn attorney and that he could help Qadira. He said that burn injury cases could be complex and he knew about these things. To this day I still do not know where Scott came from but I suspect someone sent him our way.

So by the end of May we had decided to switch Qadira's representation from Stephen P Riedlinger of Susak & Powell to Scott Kocher and Richard Vangelisti. Scott made time to come out to our house and meet Renee and I and for some reason he had reminded me of my Uncle Chris. He was white, tall, thin and very professional. He came over in a smart looking suit. He was young and he seemed to have a lot of experience. He had gone to Harvard and he impressed us with his qualifications. He seemed very confident that he was the attorney for us. He said that he was a special burn attorney and that burn injury cases were complicated. He spent a long time talking with us just making conversation and explaining his process.

By the time he left we felt confident that he was the best attorney for Qadira. After all Susak & Powell wasn't on the same par as Vangelisti Kocher LLP. They were more of a car accident law firm. We needed someone far more experienced. It was a no brainer.

Scott Kocher really made us feel like he could take charge of the situation. Now finally we wouldn't have anything to worry about when it came to Qadira's situation and at the time that was what we desperately needed. Our lives had been turned upside down and Scott's "I've got this covered" demeanor was refreshing.

His presence was going to make dealing with the insurance company a lot easier. Next time Beth Phipps showed up we wouldn't be all alone and Scott would know what to do. The entire circumstance was already very uncomfortable to talk about and it felt easier to communicate with someone more our age. He told us about some cases he had settled for burn victims and he said he would be willing to take the case on a contingency fee. We had never been in this type of situation before and we just wanted to make sure that we were handling things the right way. It appeared that Scott F. Kocher was the man for the job.

So now every month Renee had to take Qadira to Scott's office and he would take pictures of her leg. Scott acted like everything was just fine. He said that he would handle everything. He had graduated from Harvard Law School and he had a confident demeanor. He would spend a lot of time on the phone with us acting like he cared and to tell you the truth we bought it hook, line, and sinker. SLAP, KICK, PUNCH!

We trusted Scott with our daughter and we trusted Scott with ourselves. He seemed like a real professional and he had a good track record. He made us feel that he was taking care of everything and that was a relief because things at home were very stressful. We were just so happy to have Scott working for Qadira. We were still dealing with the aftermath of Qadira's burn, Kamaya was not well, and things at Nike were extremely stressful for Renee. It was a lot.

JUSTICE FOR QADIRA

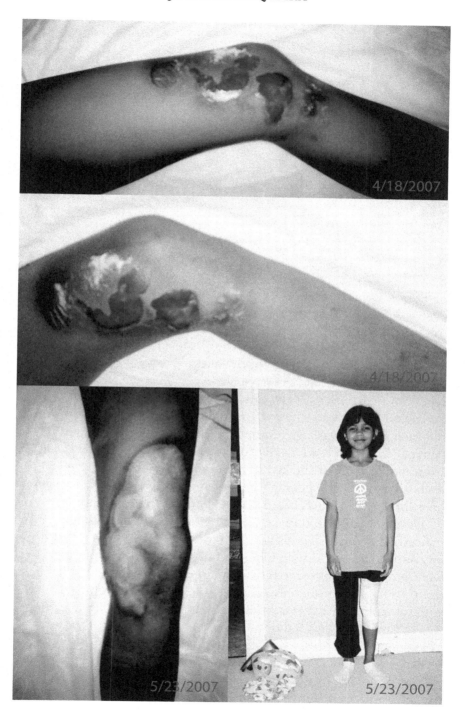

THE JOB SITUATION

Renee was feeling a lot of pressure from work. Things had really changed ever since he complained. People were acting different towards him and they were taking work off his desk. He was starting to feel really worried about his job but he just kept going to work, avoiding Randy, and hoping for the best.

In June of 2007 Mac still gave him a good review which was a relief but there was still no word from the EEOC. We didn't understand what was taking them so long to start the investigation but then again it was a government agency. We were trying to be patient. In mid-July we were excited when a woman finally called from the EEOC but she just wanted to know if Renee wanted to drop his charge. We couldn't understand why they would ask him if he wanted to drop his charge before they did an investigation.

Despite Mac's good review Renee had become increasingly concerned about losing his job. Things had gotten really weird since he complained and although he tried to give each situation the benefit of the doubt something didn't feel right. We both still felt like the charge was the only protection he had and dropping it without an investigation didn't seem to smart. Especially since Renee was still working with Randy.

At the time we were both still very hopeful that after the investigation he would be moved away from Randy. So why drop the charge? Why not just wait? After all Matthew had said they couldn't fire him, or demote him or change his position in anyway or that would be considered retaliation. What if he dropped the charge and then they fired him the next day? We couldn't survive without the income from his job. The investigation should only serve to help our situation so Renee told the EEOC that he didn't want to drop the charge.

And on August 11th 2007 instead of an investigation Renee was verbally "laid off" from his 8 year career at Nike without any comment or resolution from the EEOC. SLAP, KICK, PUNCH! Claire Hamill who was the President and CEO of Exeter called him in for a meeting that was also attended by his manager Mac and Mary Brunke from HR.

Renee was surprised when he entered the conference room that day since Claire's assistant had only mentioned "a quick touch- base" in her email. Renee actually thought he finally might be getting some good news but when he stepped into the room he could feel the tension crackling in the air. Mac, Mary and Claire were clearly having trouble containing their laughter. Renee walked in and sat down. Claire looked and him and said "you're going to have to find a new job." Her tone was cold and dismissive. He was shocked.

She continued to inform Renee that "all NASCAR positions were being eliminated" and that his position would be eliminated with them. SLAP, KICK, PUNCH! Renee looked around the room for the something that was so funny trying to gather his thoughts. What was Claire talking about? He was an Exeter Footwear designer supporting all aspects of the business. He had only recently become associated with the NASCAR initiative as a result of Randy's insane behavior but he was never one to start an argument.

He did the only thing he could think of to do at the time and thanked them for the opportunity. He stood up and shook their hands and politely informed them of the other categories at Nike where he would like to work. Maybe this was just some kind of mistake? But when he met with Mary Brunke the next day she rudely informed him that he should be looking for work outside of Nike. SLAP, KICK, PUNCH! Something was terribly wrong and he couldn't afford to lose his job like this. The timing for all of this couldn't be worse.

When he came home he immediately called Matthew Cleman to tell him what had happened. Matthew had said that Nike could not legally do this to him! The EEOC should be able to stop this from happening. The company was not supposed to be able to change his terms of employment until the initial charge had been resolved. Doing so meant breaking anti-retaliation laws.

But Renee still wasn't completely sure if there had been some kind of mistake. He wanted to think better of the company that he had given 8 years of his life to but Mary's tone and expression echoed in his ears. Matthew informed him that he could file additional charges of retaliation if he was really being fired but suddenly it didn't seem like he was going to be able to stop it from happening. The EEOC hadn't even gotten around to investigating the first charge. The entire circumstance was incredibly stressful.

Nobody had even bothered to give him a formal termination letter so he emailed Mary and asked if she could get that to him. He kept his fingers crossed that this was just some kind of mix up? All he had wanted was to be moved away from Randy. What was the big deal? Was he really truly being fired for filing a charge of discrimination? And on August 26th 2007 our worst fears were confirmed when Melissa Marks who was the Employee Relations Director for Nike emailed Renee a formal termination letter. His last day was going be September 28th so he basically got a 30 day notice. It was so FUCKING stressful!

He applied for several jobs within the company but suddenly no one would talk to him. He requested a copy of his personnel file to see if something in it was affecting his chances at getting a new job and on August 28th he received a copy which was missing the last four years of his reviews and other documents. Real mature, right? He had always gotten great reviews and luckily he had copied all of them. But someone obviously had it out for him. There was absolutely no documentation about what had occurred with Randy. So on August 29th he filed a formal charge of retaliation with the EEOC in a desperate attempt to protect his job and our family.

As the days ticked by he met with several business leads at Nike and sent out his resume to Nike directors and recruiters he had met along the way but suddenly nobody could help him. Ted Balderree told him that they were having trouble finding places for "people with degrees" and a temp flippantly told him "you're just going to have to get used to losing your job." Another colleague asked him if he was up there "stealing designs."

Everyone he had met throughout the years turned on him with a vengeance. The insults and below the belt comments were all over the place. Things were happening hard and fast. SLAP, KICK, PUNCH! People began lashing out at him. Blow after blow! It hurt like hell just to watch him endure it. Our life was just sort of unraveling right in front of our eyes and to top it all off we were in the midst of back to school with the kids. But the things I used to focus on were suddenly completely meaningless. It's hard to care about mundane everyday things when your livelihood is being ripped away. I just wanted to lie down and die.

But I was still trying hard to fit into my surroundings because obviously I wasn't dead. When my neighbors stopped to chat I had to pretend that everything was okay. I mean what else could I do? Everyone knew about the burn and that was already weird enough. I wasn't about to start announcing that Renee got fired, but unable to cope with the hostile environment he had finally just stopped going to work and probably the neighbors were starting to perceive that. We don't even think anyone at Nike noticed or cared. SLAP, KICK, PUNCH! He had basically been run out of there with pitchforks and knives.

I would try to get through each conversation without bothering anybody with my problems. I slapped on a smile and just pretended everything was fine. When People on this planet say "How are you" they don't really want to know. People are well trained to pretend that everything is okay because we all know there is not much anybody can do for us. This world doesn't stop or even slow down when people lose their normal. I would put on a brave smile and give them the highlights. Kymani was getting ready to transition out of preschool to kindergarten where he would join Qadira in the Odyssey Program. Kamaya and Qayden would be going back to preschool at Tigard Learning Center. Everyone was perfectly fine. Everything was okay. Brave smile Karellen, brave smile.

I wasn't going to stand there telling everyone that Renee had been fired and that I was sick to my stomach that Qadira was going back to school with Sophie; that I had no idea how I was going to afford my life; that Qadira's leg was completely disfigured. It was very clear that I wasn't supposed to be having those kinds of problems and if I was I certainly wasn't supposed to be talking about it. Nobody wanted to hear all that. And at this point nothing had been resolved. Renee had heard no news of a job and just the thought of running into Todd and Aimee made my stomach feel like it was headed for my shoes. Renee's daily presence and the mottled patch of skin covering a large portion of Qadira's left leg was a constant reminder that we were in the middle of a storm.

I was surprised to see the announcement in the paper in Early September that Nike was launching a strategic Review of its Exeter Brands group. Please feel free to Google that. We had the inside scoop on that so of course it caught my eye. Renee hadn't had his last day yet. Technically Renee was still officially employed with Exeter. It seemed odd right on the heels of the NASCAR divestment and nobody told Renee anything about it. The only person to contact Renee since he had stopped going to work was Mary Brunke and she just wanted to make sure he was going to be signing the severance agreement. She didn't ask why he had stopped coming to the office. Nobody did.

But unfortunately for us the severance agreement presented a huge problem because Matthew had informed Renee that if he signed the agreement then his charges would be void. He couldn't risk signing the severance agreement and losing all of his rights but on the other hand we could use the money. But then again it was only 20,000 dollars. With our lifestyle that money would be gone in a just a few months, and then what? Renee could not afford to be out of work for long before we would be destitute. And ultimately we felt that he would at least prevail on his charge of retaliation if not both charges. The case was cut and dry and the severance agreement only offered us a small temporary cushion. At this point we had no idea when or where he would be working again. But we both expected the EEOC to hurry up and put a stop to all of this. Matthew had told us that Nike could not get away with doing this. Renee emailed Mary and told her that "no severance agreement would be necessary." We felt that he had a solid case with the EEOC. It was our best chance for a fair resolution.

The very next day Lisa Olivia (Nike Design Recruiter) emailed him encouraging him to apply for a footwear design position that required a degree. Renee did not have a degree and he had already applied for multiple positions within the company that did not require a degree and he hadn't even managed to get an interview for any one of those positions. He couldn't even secure an interview for a Color Design 2 position, a job he should have been offered years ago. What was Lisa trying to do?

Her assistant Andrew Croll emailed Renee again and told him to fill out the online application and to make sure to answer "yes" to all of the qualifying questions. When Renee opened up the application and started filling it in he realized, that one of the qualifying questions that he had to answer was, do you have a degree? SLAP, KICK, PUNCH! He certainly couldn't answer "yes" to that. Lying on an application was a serious offense that he could immediately be fired for.

Renee had met Lisa and she knew he didn't have a degree. She was the recruiter he had worked with when he got the job at Exeter. Something was wrong. He emailed Lisa back telling her that he was "no longer looking for opportunities at Nike at this time." He didn't know what else to say. A friend of his had warned him that Nike was going to "crush him like a cockroach" when he told him what had been happening at Exeter. His friend's prediction had been correct. Nike had obviously chosen to destroy him.

Thank God there were protections for people like us. The feds were on the way. Any minute the investigators would show up at Nike and put a stop to all of this. A favorable determination would mean Nike would have to give Renee his job back. After all, he had been laid off with an open EEOC charge pending. How could that not be considered retaliation? It should have been an open and shut case but Renee's last day at Nike came and went with still no word from the EEOC.

MOUNTAINS OF STRESS TO CLIMB

Qadira was already having a terrible beginning to her 3rd grade year. All the kids at school knew about what had happened and she was struggling to make new friends. She had missed a lot of school after she was burned the year before and had fallen behind in math and was having a lot of trouble catching up. It was all just terrible. She was obviously very stressed out and she would cry over her homework and other little things. She had grown more soft-spoken and introverted. On her 9th birthday she had a major breakdown on the porch just crying and crying. We brought her a hamster to cheer her up that day. We didn't know what else to do.

Her leg looked horrible and it was hard to imagine what she was going through. There was a lot of tension in the house yet we were still trying to go through the motions: work, school, life, and family. It always felt like way too much. It was hard to do anything with all the dark clouds hanging over our house.

Renee was constantly looking for work in his industry but he couldn't get much of a response from anyone much less any kind of interview. He got phone interviews with Puma and Under Armor and they both acted super excited and then he never heard back from either. It was becoming pretty clear that he wasn't going to be working in the footwear industry anymore. It was terrifying trying to wrap our minds around our new reality.

Were we going to lose everything? What about the house and the kids? We were always wondering what we could have done to deserve this? I started working more hours at Benchview to make ends meet. Life had suddenly become this really super difficult thing that we didn't really care to do anymore. Renee applied for multiple jobs but his job history seemed to have dried up and disappeared. Nobody called him back and nobody would hire him. All of the friends he had made along the way deserted him. SLAP, KICK, PUNCH! After 6 years at Adidas and 8 years at Nike he was unemployable. The days crawled by and still no word from the EEOC. Then in late October Kamaya got sick.

All I can remember is the fever. She was so hot and her lymph nodes had swollen up and were poking out of the side of her neck. They told me at the clinic that she had the Cat Scratch Fever but the antibiotics didn't help and she broke out into a rash all over her body. She was losing weight. The fever was climbing all the way up to 104 and sometimes over that. After a few days I was sure she was dying.

The palms of her hands and feet had turned strawberry red along with her tongue and she barely moved. Her pale skin was clammy to the touch and her usually live mass of dark curls was matted down close by her face. She lay on the couch quiet and still. I had to keep giving her ibuprofen and Tylenol combined just to keep the fever down for a couple of hours. I knew that this couldn't go on much longer. I felt like I was killing her by pumping her full of so much medicine. After 5 days Renee headed to Emanuel Hospital seeking answers.

That evening Kamaya was diagnosed with Kawasaki's Syndrome which is a rare autoimmune disorder. She was admitted to the hospital right away. Kawasaki's Syndrome is fatal if not treated aggressively after it is discovered. In just a few days the virus would attack her heart causing lifetime damage or death. I remember Renee coming home and then me going to the hospital. Someone had to watch the kids and someone had to be with Kamaya. Again we were all alone. And the next day the hospital wanted insurance and that was a problem because we didn't have any anymore.

Renee hadn't been out of work long enough for the kids to qualify for Oregon Health Plan and the cost of covering our Cobra Health insurance was going to be an additional 1,000 dollars a month so we had decided not to sign up. Refusing to sign the severance agreement had come with consequences we had not foreseen. Renee had had to relinquish his retirement account if we hoped to survive and the penalty for taking it out early had been very steep. It had already cost us 20,000 dollars just to get the remaining 40,000 out of his retirement. The mortgage of 1,800 dollars a month was already killing us and an extra 1,000 dollar a month payment to Cobra was going to be devastating but we had to do something.

The hospital wasn't going to treat Kamaya if we didn't come up with some kind of insurance. Can you believe that? They had the medicine right outside the door but first they wanted to make sure we could pay. In this cold harsh world the paper always comes first and we needed to find a way to come up with some. Our 4 year old daughter was dying in her little hospital bed and there we were trying to come up with enough money to save her life. I was listening to Renee making calls to the Cobra provider to see if we could still sign up. What if they said no? I felt strange like I was me but I wasn't me. I was in a dream being myself and somehow whatever happened I needed to accept the outcome of this. I was in a whole new world.

Everything was completely surreal. I couldn't freak out in the hospital room. I had to stay calm and not think about an outcome that I had no control over. Smile at the doctor's, watch TV with the kids, act like everything is fine. Breathe or stop breathing. Did it really matter anymore? My body was still breathing but I was lost. They couldn't just give her the medicine? SLAP, KICK, PUNCH! What kind of world was this? I had to take a walk outside of myself and put my trust in something I couldn't see or feel.

Where was God? I couldn't make anybody do anything. It was the strangest sort of feeling. But when Renee finally got off the phone he had some good news. There was still time by just a few days. We were going to be able to squeeze in under the wire. OH THANK YOU GOD!! He just had to go give them some money and show the hospital proof of insurance. Time was running out and he rushed off to go save Kamaya the only way we knew how.

When they finally hooked her up to the medicine we tried to remain hopeful. It didn't seem like our family could endure such a loss and live to tell the tale. She had one dose but it was ineffective. Please God Please! I prayed silently in my head. I didn't know what was going to happen if she didn't make it. I felt unusually calm. Renee and I never left her side.

We took turns running back and forth to the house to take care of the other kids who couldn't be at the hospital all of the time. When they administered a second dose things started to turn around.

Kamaya had a male nurse named Joshua who called himself the "baby healer." He was full of energy and personality and he made an impression on me such that I would remember him years later in Qadira's hospital room raising my suspicions and helping to uncover yet another terrible secret. The story was being written right before my very eyes.

Kamaya spent just a little over a week in the hospital recovering. When we brought her home she wasn't much of herself anymore. She was thin and frail and we worried that she would get sick again. She was only 22 pounds when they discharged her. A bag of little bones. It didn't matter how well I bundled her up, on cold days her lips and fingers would turn blue. My brother Uranus who was staying with us while he went through his divorce helped out by watching Kamaya whenever she wasn't feeling well. We certainly could use the help.

I was also very worried about Qadira who had developed a funny dark rash around her mouth that was looking terrible. And Qayden was going through a terrible case of the terrible two's. I felt sorry for Kymani because I felt like I didn't have any time to be his mom anymore. I was just glad that he had his artwork to keep him busy. He had been drawing since he came out of the womb and people had taken notice. Some of his teachers even took to saving some of his work convinced that he would be famous one day. When things were bad Kymani kept a pen in his hand and he drew. And all the things we used to enjoy were disappearing faster than we could have ever imagined. It was one hell of a slippery slope and we were sliding down fast and hard. We tried to have a happy Halloween for the kids. We went through all the expected motions. Costumes, handing out candy, decorating the house but everything felt forced.

On November 17th 2007 Renee filed a third charge of defamation against Nike because he could no longer get an interview in his industry. SLAP, KICK, PUNCH! It was extremely disheartening for him to no longer be able to get even an interview. Everyone he knew turned their back on him and he didn't know anything else. He had practically grown up in the industry and with 4 kids and a wife he needed to be working. It was pretty foul how Nike had done him.

He had obviously been blacklisted from the industry. He even tried to go back to Adidas but they wouldn't even give him the time of day. All those people who had come to our wedding wouldn't lift one finger to help him. We were both beginning to spiral down into a deep depression as the days dragged by. We did our best to keep up appearances with the neighbors and the world but each day was harder than the day before. It felt like the EEOC was taking an eternity.

And November 17th also happened to be the same day that Scott called me up and told me that Aimee and Todd were being difficult and that he was advising that we file a lawsuit. This was just one headache after another. Whatever Scott thought we should do. I was in no frame of mind to be making any real decisions. He said that in order to move forward with Qadira's case that she needed a "guardian ad litem" and that I had to fill that role.

He told me that I would be the main person responsible for making decisions in Qadira's case but he would be there guiding me. I wasn't even sure what he was talking about but I was willing to do anything to help Qadira. Scott was a smart Harvard educated lawyer and I hung on his every word. He said he didn't think Renee was a suitable candidate for the job because of his dispute with Nike. Yes Scott knew everything about everything. Sometimes he would just call to talk and see how we were. We trusted him wholeheartedly.

We tried to keep things "normal." December rolled around. We were positive that Renee's job issues would be resolved once the government took a closer look at the circumstances. Renee had lost a lot of weight from the worry and stress but we still put up the Christmas tree and made sure Santa came down the chimney. We were really trying to hold it together for the kids but the outlook wasn't looking so good. What was taking the EEOC so long?

As the money continued to dwindle it felt like we were slowly bleeding to death. SLAP, KICK, PUNCH! Sometimes Renee would have long conversations with Matthew who just seemed to be very interested to know how we were "getting by." Matthew had been so very optimistic about our situation so in late January of 2008 we were shocked to receive 3 "indeterminate" findings on all of the charges Renee had filed. There was no explanation of the findings just an X in a box next to the word "indeterminate" and case closed.

So were we just supposed to accept that Renee could no longer get a job? What about the charge of retaliation? He was fired with an open EEOC charge pending. WHAT THE FUCK? What was so "indeterminate" about that? How were we going to live? My caregiving job couldn't support the family and Renee's meager retirement was running out fast. The notice said we had 90 days to file a lawsuit or lose all of our rights in the matter. Matthew disappeared, nowhere to be found. It was another harsh cold slap in the face after all the waiting we had done.

And to top that all off Qadira was really not well. Her tongue had turned a strawberry red and a dark rash around her mouth continued to persist and there were still times when she struggled to breath. On January 22nd 2008 I took her back to OHSU afraid that she was also coming down with the dreaded Kawasaki's syndrome. They ran a comprehensive metabolic test and came back to us a couple of days later insisting she just had the flu. But she didn't get any better. With nothing to really go on I began to change the family diet by pulling all of the wheat out of our diet. Maybe she was suffering from allergies? With no answers from the doctor's I decided to try something to help everyone be a little healthier. I needed something to focus on besides doom and gloom.

And then in early February while we were still trying to wrap our minds around what the EEOC had just done Scott was calling wanting to set up depositions in Qadira's case. SLAP, KICK, PUNCH! It was like a tightrope balancing act to keep getting up in the morning when each day seemed to bring more and more stress. How do you keep going when your world keeps turning upside down? Things like reading to my kids, cleaning the house, taking the kids to school, cooking dinner, sleeping, moving, breathing, it all got harder and harder and harder with each passing day.

I just didn't want to have to do it anymore. It was so hard. Simple things like walking took a tremendous amount of effort and concentration. I could literally barely make sense of what was happening anymore yet I had all this shit to deal with. I still had to go to work and take care of the old people and deal with Sala living out of his van on the side of my house and Qadira's injury and Renee's job loss. It was like being hit by a truck every single day and having to scrape my bloodied, bruised body off the side of the concrete just to get out of the middle of the road. The whole world had gone crazy and now Scott was telling me we had to schedule depositions to get Qadira's case resolved? It was just part of the process he said. Another hoop we had to jump through to make sure Qadira was taken care of.

So on February 26th 2008 I found myself at Rudy Lachenmeier's office sitting with Qadira across from Todd and Sophie who seemed to have gotten a little pudgier since I had last seen her. I didn't understand why the depositions were being held at Lachenmeier's office or why I had to sit across the table from these people but I held my tongue. People have always told me that I talk too much and I didn't want to start running my mouth and mess things up for Qadira.

Things in our life were already so bad the last thing I wanted to do was make them worse. Todd and Sophie were chatting and talking loudly which was getting on my last nerve. And where was Aimee? Everything was fun and games to those two as they sat there bright eyed with smiles on their faces as if we were going to be discussing something pleasant and fun. I didn't like their fat attorney either. Rudy Lachenmeier was loud, rude, and obnoxious. The kind of guy the barrels around like a bull in china shop. I just wanted to get this over with and get myself and my daughter out of here.

Lachenmeier asked Todd and Sophie to step into another room and Aimee suddenly came into the room. She sat at the end of the table staring at me and Qadira. SLAP, KICK, PUNCH! My stomach was in knots. Now that Aimee was in the room I was wondering what she was doing here? Why was Aimee in the room? Was Aimee going to stay in the room? But I didn't feel like I could ask any questions because I had never been in a situation like this.

I kept my mouth shut and looked at Scott for answers but it was Rudy who started talking. First he started questioning Qadira. His tone of voice resembled him. Every word that dripped out of his fat mouth irritated me. His tone was boorish and insensitive. I didn't like this man talking to my daughter about anything and wanted that woman who burned my daughter out of the room. But who was I to question the process? Should I say something or keep my big mouth shut? I felt like I couldn't breathe. I didn't understand what Aimee was doing here? I watched Rudy ask my daughter all kinds of questions and each word spoken made me more and more uncomfortable.

Qadira was only nine at the time and something felt terribly wrong but she put on a brave smile trying her best to answer Rudy's questions. In my opinion the questions seemed to be all over the place. Rudy even asked Qadira if we had put something on her burn. What was that all about? What did he mean did we put something on her burn? Why would we have put something on Qadira's burn?

Qadira told Rudy the same story we had heard since she was well enough to tell it. Sophie had wanted to take a bath because she wanted to show Qadira how her parents do this "teakettle thing." Qadira had wanted to call home to ask if she could take the bath but Sophie had begged her not to afraid we would say no. When they were playing in the tub Aimee had come in with a teapot full of scalding water and the girls had stood on the lip of the tub when suddenly Todd out of nowhere came charging into the bathroom. Qadira was frightened and she tried to hide and slipped off the edge into the stream of boiling water. But she had sustained so much damage? Why had Aimee kept pouring the water after she fell? Why were the kids playing naked in the tub? There were still a lot of holes in the story that Todd and Aimee needed to fill.

As Qadira talked Aimee just sat there staring at us. Her face was all red and flushed. It was a very uncomfortable situation. I kept looking at Scott but he just sat there acting like everything was just right as rain as Rudy interrogated our daughter. I told myself that if something was wrong surely it was Scott's job to speak up but he never did so what was I to think? This was a process that I knew nothing about. Maybe I was just being paranoid about things I didn't understand. But it was a very intimidating circumstance especially with Aimee seated across the room glaring at me and my daughter and as the day went on things got even weirder.

When it was my turn Rudy started asking me a lot of personal questions that had nothing to do with Qadira's burn, but Scott kept telling me I had to answer every single question. Rudy seemed to want to know all about my life and family. What was this all about? I didn't understand why he was asking me half of the questions he was asking me but Scott kept instructing me to answer all of them no matter how off topic they seemed.

When he finally got to asking me about the burn I told him what I could. I wasn't a medical expert so there wasn't much I could tell him except what I thought he already knew. When Rudy asked me if we had put some kind of "dye" on the burn I looked at him like he was crazy. What was this man talking about? Why would we have put dye on Qadira's burn? Was this man insane? I looked at Scott but he just sat there doing nothing.

At one point near the end Rudy asked me if Qadira had been sexually abused. I was so shocked I could hear my heart thudding loudly in my chest. What the hell was this guy talking about? I couldn't even believe what had just come out of this man's mouth! I looked at Scott searching his face for some kind of answer but he just acted like everything was fine. "Answer the question" Scott said. I was so confused, my mouth was dry and I felt covered in a cold sweat. Aimee's eyes were boring into me from across the room. I answered Rudy's question to the best of my knowledge. "No" I said firmly. I couldn't believe what had just happened.

After that I was anxious to get out of there as fast as I could. Scott took me out in the hall and told me that he would handle Todd, Aimee, and Sophie's depositions by himself so it wasn't necessary for me to stay. Being in the presence of those people and talking about what happened had made me feel very angry and confused. I was mad at Scott but somehow glad he was there to take over.

I kept telling myself that there was a process and I just had to get through it. Scott was Qadira's attorney, he had a great track record, and he had always been nice to our family. I had no reason to distrust him but something about this experience that I couldn't quite put my finger on had left me feeling violated. I told myself that it was the circumstance that made me feel this way. Driving home I felt shaky and sick. Why did Aimee have to burn up Qadira? Why God? Why? All I could do was keep wishing that the burn didn't happen but every day I kept waking up in the same recurring nightmare and it was about to get even worse.

Renee had started talking to attorney's after we got our "right to sue" from the EEOC. He only had 90 days to file suit or he would lose all of his rights in the matter. For our family that was equal to a death sentence. 90 days wasn't a lot of time and he was frantically trying his hardest to get some representation. He talked to all the attorneys that he could find but nobody would help him. In fact most of the attorney's he talked to spent ample time trying to discourage him from going after Nike.

We were learning a very powerful lesson because this is what happens when big business owns a state. They can do whatever they want because in reality they "own" the entire attorney's in town. It must have been some kind of unspoken rule because they all abided by it. You don't bite the hand that feeds you. SLAP, KICK, PUNCH! It was much easier just to turn Renee into the sacrificial lamb than risk going up against a company like Nike. We couldn't even find an out of state attorney to take the case and we called everybody. But we knew we had to somehow file a lawsuit. What else were we going to do? We had a right to sue and the EEOC hadn't figured anything out. We had to have our day in court because Nike had decided to take everything. We were getting thrown out with the trash. We were almost out of money and our family was heading straight to the welfare line. We had no choice but to fight this.

Sometimes the attorney's would yell at Renee insisting that he had no case. It was very discouraging. But he was determined to get us some help. The case against Nike was so cut and dry we both had a hard time believing that we wouldn't win in court. They had laid Renee off while he had an open EEOC charge pending and Randy had basically admitted to what he had done. This should have been easily resolved by the EEOC and why we couldn't find an attorney was beyond both of us? Renee looked and looked.

Every single day he called and searched for help. One attorney bluntly stated "I know what they are doing is wrong but it's Nike." It was becoming increasingly clear that Nike was king. The quest seemed futile but Renee was determined to turn over every rock desperate to find someone who could help him. He had spent his whole life in the Footwear industry and now it was all going to be ripped away because Randy couldn't keep his hands to himself and he had complained? It didn't seem fair at all. And then in early May just weeks before we needed to get the suit filed Mitra Shari walked into our life.

Mitra was the Hollywood of attorney's. She was hair, nails, jewelry, and perfume. The glamour girl of employment law. She made us feel like finally we had someone in our corner. Her middle eastern accent and sassy demeanor gave her flair. She was the picture of confidence. It seemed like a match made in heaven when she walked into the room. We were so grateful that someone had finally taken the case. Finally, someone who cared and just in the nick of time. Thank God! We were really starting to believe that we were going to have to do this on our own. And she assured us that our case was solid. Mitra was going to be our hero. When we handed her all the paperwork all she could say was "I can't believe it, it's all here." And she was right.

There had been no reason for the EEOC's indeterminate finding except for the "fat white envelope" that we secretly began to suspect had tainted Matthew's decision. But much to our relief Mitra and her trusty sidekick Adam Weiner were going to get the job done. After all; the law was on our side. When I met Mitra she had hugged me like a sister and for once I felt reassured that everything was going to be okay. The judge would see this case for what it was and we would get our life back.

After Mitra took the case Scott called telling me we had to attend a mediation to try to settle Qadira's claim. We had talked a few times since the depositions and he had assured me that everything was going as it should. Once again I was thrust into a situation that I knew nothing about. I found myself in a high rise in downtown with a tall, thin man by the name of John Barker. And fat rude Rudy was there and two other men I didn't know. They asked to see Qadira's scar and Mr. Barker leered towards Qadira. "Hey Qadira" he said as he slid his pant leg up his calf showing her what they were expecting her to do. What the hell was this man doing? I put my arm around my daughter to shield her and looked at Scott. Why wasn't he saying anything to this man? I felt scared and confused again.

That sick feeling that had overcome me during the depositions was back. I had to speak up. "Don't scare her." I quickly interjected giving Mr. Barker a disapproving glance. He straightened up but he didn't say sorry. And now Scott was instructing Qadira to show the men her scar and there was an uncomfortable silence as she complied. Why would he make her do this? State Farm had plenty of pictures. SLAP, KICK, PUNCH! We had put our trust in Scott but something about the process wasn't feeling right again.

I wanted to do more to protect my daughter from all of this but I didn't feel like I had the authority to question Scott's knowledge. He was her attorney. He had gone to Harvard and I was just a high school graduate but why did he just make Qadira do that in front of all those people? Hadn't she been put through enough? What about what had happened at the depositions? But then I would think about all the nice phone conversations we had had and I would convince myself that Scott was just doing what had to be done. I was being paranoid and overprotective. I told myself to keep my big mouth shut. Scott cared about Qadira and he knew what he was doing. I wasn't about to start questioning his expertise when I knew nothing about the process.

We were then ushered into a small office and Mr. Barker began explaining jury verdicts as if I could understand what he was talking about. Then he would leave the room for a while and then he would come back and throw out some random numbers 3000, 7000, 10,000. And Scott would counsel me not to take anything. He kept telling me that their offers were ridiculous. I had no idea what I was doing so I was trying to do my best to listen to everything that was said. How could I determine the impact of what had happened to Qadira or how the experience or the scar would affect her life? Scott kept reminding me that as Qadira's "guardian ad litem" that I had to make the final decision. I felt like it was all on me. There was so much pressure.

And Renee had to leave right in the middle of the mediation to go to work. He had finally found a job welding for Gunderson. It wasn't shoe design but it was a paycheck. It started at 14 dollars per hour. It was a mere fraction of what he had been making at Nike but at least there would be something trickling in. And here was Mr. Barker again offering 17,000 dollars, then Scott telling me again that I shouldn't take it, then Mr. Barker coming in one last time saying that they "might" go up to 25,000.

When Mr. Barker left the room Scott looked me dead in the eye and said "I have never counseled a client to walk out of mediation but I am going to counsel you to walk out because these offers are totally ridiculous." I didn't know what else to do. He was the one with the Harvard education. So I did what he advised me to do and walked out of the mediation. I didn't know what I was doing there anyway so I was relieved once again to be told that I could leave. How was I supposed to put a number on this thing? Scott was the attorney and I needed to follow his lead if I wanted to do right by my daughter.

A TRIP TO HELL

The time for Renee to file the lawsuit was running out. Mitra kept telling Renee she was going to get it filed but then she just wouldn't do it. Now we had ten days left and she was calling saying she was no longer going to represent him. I could hear Renee having a heated argument with her, "Mitra." He was protesting loudly. Mitra, I don't work in my industry anymore!" He threw the phone hard against the wall. He turned to me and said "She said that my dad died and I went crazy."

His dark eyes were snapping with anger and disbelief. What were we going to do now? What the hell was that supposed to mean anyway? WHAT THE FUCK? Apparently there wasn't a shortage of fat white envelopes in this town when it came to this thing. SLAP, KICK, PUNCH! It was pretty clear someone had gotten to Mitra. We were going to have to figure out how to write a complaint and file this thing ourselves because it was times up in terms of finding another attorney. Funny how lawyers stand between us and our so called; "rights." It's like you can have the right all you want but if you can't have access to it what does it even matter? We were going to have to take a quick trip to law school if we wanted to salvage this fight.

That night as we pondered what to do next I had a very strange dream. Renee was wrapped in white cloth and was crossing a huge ocean surrounded in mist. It felt like a vision of something I could not understand. But when I woke up that morning I felt that no matter what we had to fight this thing. It was scary but I believed in my husband. I sat him down and told him he could do this. The bottom line is he was right and Nike was wrong. Any judge would be able to see that; and so started our journey into the legal system.

Renee looked up some sample complaints on the internet to fashion his complaint after. He was good on the computer, good at formatting. I was good at writing and good at arguing. His design training had served him well. My attitude had served me well. We made a pretty good team. It was incredibly nerve racking but 10 days later on June 6th 2008 Plaintiff Renee Stephens filed a lawsuit in the Washington County State Court against Nike/Exeter Brands group for sex discrimination, sexual harassment, retaliation, and defamation. The media looked the other way.

And shortly thereafter Scott was calling telling us that Fat Rudy needed to depose Renee to move Qadira's case forward. We didn't put two and two together. The deposition was scheduled for June 30th 2008. And much like my deposition Renee complained that Rudy was sure asking him a lot of personal questions. I had been wondering what had gone on because Renee had been gone all afternoon. But again Scott had made it seem like this was just standard protocol and that Renee's deposition might make the other side make an offer that we could accept. We didn't have a whole lot of time to focus on the things Scott was telling us. Due to the amount of stress we were under with the kids, the house, the pets, and our dwindling bank account we just did whatever Scott said.

At the very least a good outcome for Qadira was paramount. Scott kept telling me as we neared the trial date "oh I know Rudy; he'll probably just lean over and offer to settle for about 40,000 dollars." If that's what Scott thought then I was going to go along with it. I just listened to him and trusted him. He assured me that Qadira's case was cut and dry and he made it seem like the trial wasn't really going to happen. I believed him. The dance that he was doing with Rudy was just all part of the process. Why wouldn't I believe him? The one thing we knew for sure was that Todd and Aimee had been at the very least, negligent.

But we didn't want to put Qadira through a trial. We knew that for sure. I honestly did not think she could handle it. She had been through enough and the school year had been extremely difficult. Todd and Aimee had continued to volunteer in her class after Aimee burned up Qadira and she had had to endure the stress of seeing them at school throughout the entire ordeal. I have no idea how she did it. I personally could not stand the sight of those people but politely kept my opinion to myself thinking this would all resolve itself through the legal process.

I used to imagine ramming into Aimee's car when I saw her in car line. Those two made me sick. They just pranced around the school as if burning up our daughter had been no big deal and they seemed to have all kinds of support from the community. At least Scott had advised us that we didn't need to bring Qadira to the trial so that was a big relief.

I couldn't imagine what it would be like for her to recount that horrible night in front of those people. She had already been put through that at her deposition with Aimee staring her down. I didn't want her to have to go through that again in front of 12 strangers. We worried that an all-white jury might not be so sympathetic to Qadira's plight if she didn't attend the trial. But Scott easily disabused of that notion.

He was an experienced lawyer who had graduated from Harvard and recovered damages for cases much less cut and dry than this one. He would bring pictures of Qadira and pictures of her burn. That should certainly be plenty. He reminded us again that Todd and Aimee were already clearly negligent. The trial was just to determine damages and he calmly reassured us that everything would be fine. Why wouldn't I believe him?

On the day of the trial we told Qadira very little about what was happening. She was only 9 at the time so we didn't want to worry her. I remember feeling so small in the courtroom. Here I was a 30 year old woman with 4 children and I had never once set foot in a courtroom.

I had no idea what to expect. I was just grateful that Scott was there to guide me through the process. Judge Michael McShane had come out looking very official in the signature black robe that I had only seen on television shows. Rudy and Scott were taking care of the preliminary matters. Scott said Rudy was trying to get the photos of Qadira's burn stricken. But how could he do that?

The jury certainly needed to be able to see the extent of Qadira's injury. My heart was beating and I felt sweaty and cold. They argued and then the judge made his decision. It was a victory. The pictures were going to stay. I was thinking that maybe this whole process wouldn't be so bad.

When the jury members flooded in for jury selection I was surprised to recognize one of the jurors from Hayhurst. I believe she was the grandmother of a couple of kids in the Odyssey Program. She had a weird old face like something out of Grimm's fairytales so I spotted her right away. I told Scott and he asked me if I was bothered by her and I said "no, I guess not." I mean he was the attorney, if she wasn't supposed to be there he would tell me right?

All of the potential jurors were white just as we had feared they would be. I was a little discouraged by that. Two of the prospective jurors told stories of family members who they knew had been burned but they made sure to add that no one had ever sued anyone over it. One of the jurors, a balding guy with a shiny head kept making strange faces at me.

I thought I recognized him but I couldn't remember from where. The whole thing seemed very odd but with nothing to compare it to I just sat there telling myself that I had to trust the process. Scott busied himself asking questions and crossing people off some list he had made. I was trying to make some kind of sense of the procedure that I was witnessing but since I had never set foot in a courtroom before I wasn't sure what to think.

After Rudy and Scott made their opening statements Aimee was called up to the stand. She sat up there and told everyone that she had burned up Qadira. But now she claimed that Qadira hadn't slipped off the edge of the bathtub. Instead she claimed that Qadira had been standing behind her on the floor and that Qadira had jumped into the stream of boiling water. She was suddenly telling a story I had never heard before and she said all of this as if she believed that a kettle full of scalding water in a bathroom was just totally okay.

She said they had been playing Little House on the Prairie and she said that Qadira had had a bath at their house before. WAIT! What? What the FUCK? Did I hear that right? SLAP, KICK, PUNCH!

Then she claimed that she had called us multiple times which again was not true. WHAT WAS HAPPENING? There were phone records to prove that and I had given those to Scott. Why wasn't he contesting anything she said? Then she was saying that they had just been getting ready to take Qadira to the hospital when I came. LADY STOP LYING! STOP IT! Everything she said was a lie and Scott questioned none of it. She just sat up there and lied and Scott said nothing. And then she said she wasn't responsible for what happened to Qadira at all. So whose fault was it? What the fuck was going on? My heart was just pounding away in my chest. What was this woman saying? She was lying. Why was she lying?

I was heated when she got off the stand. My heart was pounding so hard I thought I might have a heart attack. I told Scott I wanted to talk to him right away. He took me out in the hall and said that we weren't going to make this a "pissing match." He said that it didn't matter where Qadira had been standing because Aimee was negligent regardless. He was completely calm so I tried to calm down to. But Aimee was lying. Why was Aimee telling lies?

Scott told me that none of that mattered. And I told him I had never heard about this "other" bath. He told me very calmly that everything was fine. I felt horrified and terrified all at the same time. My heart was pounding! He brushed it off and told me to stay calm. He made me feel like I was going to ruin everything for Qadira if I couldn't remain calm and at this point we didn't have much time to talk.

It was a pull yourself together moment for Karellen. I needed to focus if I wanted a good outcome for my daughter. I wished so badly that Renee was there so I could talk to him but they wouldn't let him be in the courtroom while any of us testified so he wasn't going to come until it was his turn which wasn't until tomorrow. I needed to breathe and take a step back.

This trial was just about damages and Scott reminded me again I had to stay looking nice in front of the jury. Everything was so confusing. He said it wouldn't do any good to try and make Aimee look bad. Why should we be worried about Aimee looking bad? I could hardly catch my breath. I had so many questions that I didn't know how to ask and the clock was ticking so fast.

I wanted so badly to do right by Qadira, and Scott was telling me my attitude in front of the jury was going to ruin things for her. Scott was Qadira's attorney and of course he was doing his job. I needed to stop being paranoid about everything but still something seemed very very wrong. There just wasn't any time for me to think and Scott was already ushering me back into the courtroom. Everything was a huge blur.

When I got on the stand Rudy let into me hard. First things first he wanted the jury to know that I wasn't employed. His words were cold and hard. He wanted to know if I thought Qadira had changed in any way since the burn. He wanted to know what her teachers and our neighbors thought about changes in her personality since she was burned. He was asking questions that I couldn't even answer. How could I tell him what someone else thought? He asked about the meaning of Qadira's name and if she had a best friend in Tigard. Qadira didn't have a best friend in Tigard. What was this guy talking about?

He asked a ton of irrelevant questions that seemed geared at painting me as an unreasonable person. At one point I even found myself saying out loud "I don't see how that's relevant." I couldn't see what he was doing but I could feel it. He seemed to be attacking me as hard as he could and even made the suggestion that I had taken too long getting Qadira to the hospital because I had chosen to take her to Providence hospital. Even Judge McShane had to jump in to remind the jury that failure to get quick medical care wasn't a claim. What was happening?

Then Rudy was throwing some more irrelevant questions at me about some disagreements that we had had with some neighbors that had nothing to do with Qadira being burned and making a big ass deal out of them. He was literally comparing Qadira's burn to some petty disagreements that had nothing to do with anything. Like Qadira's burn had been no big deal and we had just sued Todd and Aimee because we were shitty people. I felt completely alone. Scott said nothing. I felt like I felt during the depositions. I could barely breathe. SLAP, KICK, PUNCH!

The jury was giving me some pretty unforgiving looks but maybe that was just my imagination running wild. My heart was pounding hard in my chest. Everyone had been super nice to Aimee when they had questioned her. What the hell was going on? Again it seemed that Scott wasn't doing much lawyering. He was so quiet. He could barely seem to eke out an objection now and again. But again this was my first trial so it was hard for me to see what was happening. All I had to go on was how I felt and somehow I felt like I was suddenly on trial.

After my testimony was done Rudy's assistant Betsy Fernley was called to the stand by Rudy to read Qadira's deposition. I listened to her drone away and butcher our kid's names but I was glad Qadira was somehow there in spirit. The sound of her words comforted me. Her voice came through strong in the deposition and surely the jury would take note that Aimee had been lying about what happened. Her version of what happened and Qadira's version were different. Qadira had been standing on the lip of the tub and she had never had a bath at their house before and she had told Rudy so in her deposition.

Certainly the jury would see through Aimee's assertion that this was somehow Qadira's fault. I couldn't even understand how they could be making that assertion. It was Preposterous! Scott had done nothing to prepare me for what I was now being subjected to. SLAP, KICK, PUNCH! He had never once told me that Aimee and Todd were taking no responsibility for what had happened. It seemed like Rudy's whole angle was that Qadira's injury was no big deal.

And when it came time to put pictures of Qadira's burn on the projection machine Scott suddenly couldn't get his computer to work so he said he couldn't do it. I felt very upset when this happened but I didn't know what to say. He gave the jury some pictures of the burn to look at but I couldn't tell which ones he gave them because he had put a bunch of photos in identical looking folders. Some of the folders just contained pictures of Qadira after she was burned and some of them contained pictures of her burn at different stages. I couldn't get a good sense of anything that was happening in front of me.

On day two I had to watch Todd sit up there and tell the jurors that he knew all about burns and that Qadira's burns hadn't been that bad. Excuse me but Todd was not a doctor. What the fuck did he know? He hadn't dealt with Qadira's burn injury, we had! He hadn't changed her bandages, we had! Who was he? He said that the reason the girls were naked is because they were playing "Little house on the prairie" and that he played that game with Sophie all the time. What the hell? Who does that? What was all this sudden talk of "Little house on the prairie?" Rudy had even opened with that assertion when he had made his opening statement and Scott had followed suit in his.

This whole thing was making me feel very upset and confused. Todd talked about how it was him who boiled up the kettle and gave it to Aimee. He said that he was sure that Qadira had taken a bath at their house before on another occasion. SLAP, KICK, PUNCH!

Then he talked about his master's degree and where he worked and how he volunteered all the time up at the school and how he thought I hadn't gotten Qadira to the hospital fast enough. WHAT THE FUCK? Suddenly everyone was acting like I hadn't taken Qadira's burn injury seriously. WHAT THE HELL WAS GOING ON? Things were happening so fast and it was one big blur and they were saying so many things I had never heard before. Rudy even played some video of Qadira dancing at an Odyssey Program function.

When Renee finally took the stand Scott asked him a bunch of questions about Qadira's burn and our care of the wound. He made sure to ask Renee where he had been working at the time. "Nike" he replied. And then there were superficial questions about what Renee thought Qadira felt about her injury. On the cross examination Rudy made sure to ask what my husband was doing for work currently like that had anything to do with the fact that Aimee had burned up Qadira. "Unemployed" he replied. They were painting one nasty picture. SLAP, KICK, PUNCH! He asked about whom Qadira's teachers at school were; and brought up other irrelevant information he had gathered along the way. Mostly he asked about the same issues that we had had with our neighbors that he had asked me about that had nothing to do with the burn or Todd or Aimee. Scott never said a word. It all seemed very out of place.

Sophie was the last to testify all dressed up in her new yellow shoes. She also claimed that Qadira had taken a bath at their house before. My blood boiled in my ears! She talked about how Qadira had been crying that night to go home and how her mother had burned Qadira. She said Qadira wanted to take a bath to wash off because she was allergic to cats which was totally not true. I was so confused at this point. There were so many things being said that I had never heard before. I needed some time to process. I didn't understand why Sophie was even there. Wasn't this trial supposed to be about the fact that Todd and Aimee had burned up Qadira? Scott hadn't prepared me for any of this. I was at a complete loss.

And suddenly the jury was filing back into the jury room laughing really loudly. SLAP, KICK, PUNCH! A huge shock to my system. Why were they laughing? WHY WERE THEY LAUGHING? WHAT THE FUCK? What was so funny? What the fuck was so funny? I could feel hot tears streaming down my face. What about looking at pictures of my burned up daughter was so funny? I was just standing there encased in a cloud of confusion and I felt like my heart would pound its way out of my chest and land on the floor in front of me. The lead juror was called to read the verdict and she faced me with a horrifically nasty expression on her face. I knew she was going to deliver bad news. She looked like the Devil incarnate. Evil and ugly as hell...

Scott had warned us over and over to have no reaction when the verdict was read and I was trying to remain calm but something evil seemed to be taking up all the space in the room. "We the jury find the defendant not negligent and it was unanimous!" That word "unanimous" it hurt so bad like nails on a chalkboard. It was a unified front. I was sick, sick, sick! Susan Glosser's voice had a piercing accusatory tone and she looked at me as if to say "that's what you get." It was a harsh blow to the gut.

I could hear ringing in my ears and I struggled to breath. It was quiet where my mind went and my body was enveloped by a strange energy as if someone had just covered me in an invisible blanket. I couldn't see Renee but for him he said it was like a loud "pop" and then a deep silence. And then the judge was talking. I was back in reality and I started to scream Qadira's name. I couldn't contain myself and I ran out of the courtroom. I heard Renee come out after me. He grabbed me and hugged me tight like the night of our car accident so long ago. He dried my eyes. He calmed me down and reassured me. We sat on the bench outside of the courtroom. Neither of us wanted to hear anymore.

Fat Rudy came out first. He forcefully said we should have thought about what we had done to the Burkholder's. I hated him. I hated his fat mouth, fat red face, and loud ugly voice. He bellowed "Do you have any idea what you did to them." What we did to them? What did we do to them? What the fucking hell was he talking about? Then Todd and Aimee came out of the courtroom and I felt so much anger and sadness at the same time that it was hard to stay upright on the bench. I hated them. I wanted both of them to die.

I hated Todd's mealy mouthed slimy demeanor. I wanted to bash Aimee's head into the floor. My stomach was in knots. I couldn't even move. I was just sitting there feeling like someone had just put ten thousand pounds on my shoulders. I was glad when they disappeared down the stairs out of my sight. And then Scott was there acting apologetic. He said that Todd and Aimee had about 8,000 dollars of attorney's fees that we "owed" them but that he could probably work something out with Rudy since Renee was just a welder. SLAP, KICK, PUNCH!

It was pure torture of the worst kind. And Scott took it upon himself to remind me that this was my entire fault. I had been Qadira's "guardian ad litem" he said, and I had made the final decision to come to a trial. I thought I must be going insane. Was Scott really sitting there telling me that we "owed" Todd and Aimee money for burning up Qadira? What the hell? What was even happening? This had not been what I had expected at all and suddenly I was being told that I was responsible for the whole thing.

It's all "your" fault Scott reminded me. And I was left questioning myself. Had I, as Qadira's "guardian ad litem" done something wrong? I wanted to die. Please God just let me die! I begged the universe to kill me. I wanted the floor to open up and swallow me whole. I felt drained. I couldn't think or talk. My body was breathing but I couldn't feel anything. I wanted to disappear but I didn't know how. I needed to get home. I didn't want Scott's apologies and I didn't want to hear the "I'm so sorry" from his assistant. I didn't understand what had happened in that courtroom.

When I got home Uranus's friend Zora happened to be waiting for my brother on our front porch. I just wanted to be left alone to die. What did this mean for us and for our daughter? She would have to live with the horror of that night for the rest of her life and somehow I had managed to fuck it all up for her. I had somehow made sure through my own stupidity that she got nothing. How could I have done that to her? Why and how did I walk out of that mediation? And Renee was right beside me kicking himself over and over. Why did he let Qadira go over to their house that night? He hated himself for what he felt he had caused. If only he had said no! Over and over he kept repeating that.

But there was Zora telling us that things happen for a reason. She was telling me that I had to trust that God had a plan. I didn't know Zora very well but I sure am grateful that she was on my porch that day. She gave me that little bit of strength that I needed to keep breathing. I needed something that day and just her presence was enough. My mind was trying to sort out what I had just witnessed and make some sense out of it but the more we talked it over the less sense we could make. And what was this bath Sophie and Todd had been talking about? I was so scared to even think about it. It made my heart go numb inside my chest. Qadira had no recollection of ever taking a bath at the Burkholder house. I had seen the Butterfly Effect. Was this someone's idea of a sick joke? What the fuck was happening? What the hell really happened on the night of April 12th 2007? Did Qadira really even remember what happened to her? We decided to call the police.

Officer Westberry showed up at our door with an attitude. He insisted loudly to us that we were not allowed to make a police report about what had happened. He was just another doughnut eating, fat, sweaty, white cop. We told him we most certainly could make a police report but he refused to take one. He seemed angry that we had even called. Like what was it to him if we wanted to make a report. Why wouldn't he do his job? After he left my heart was beating outside of my chest. This had turned into one hell of a day and I didn't feel like I could take much more.

My friend Anise called the next day and invited us swimming at her apartment and I decided to take her up on it. The situation was fucked and after yelling at the stupid fat cop yesterday I just needed to gather my nerves. What year was this anyway? What did he mean we couldn't file a report? I remember sitting in the pool staring at Qadira feeling like every part of me was dying.

The long dark scar on her leg stood out as a stark reminder of everything that had happened. I was so sad that I thought that I might break in two pieces. It was work to breath. Anise was smiling and cheerful and I wished I could inject some of that life into my heart so it could start beating at its normal rate again. I couldn't feel anything anymore. The world was happening without me in it. My body was sitting out in the sun next to Anise's swimming pool while the rest of me had taken refuge in a place where the pain could not get close enough to kill me.

JUSTICE FOR QADIRA

That night I had a very vivid dream. It was misty in my house and we had a pet King Cobra. My family was all laying on our king sized bed and we were letting the snake slither all over us. We were petting the snake and holding it as if it was a part of the family. And then suddenly we were in the living room and we were all looking for the snake. I saw Qadira go towards the back room. I called out to her but she didn't seem to hear me. She was wearing her little turquoise pajama bottoms and a thin white t-shirt. She opened up the back door and ran down our back steps. I called out to her again. I didn't want her to go outside because it was so cold but she didn't seem to hear me. She was transfixed on something and I realized the snake had her attention. He had reared up in front of the open garage door and they seemed to be conversing.

I couldn't move from my position on the top step. This went on for some time and then the snake reared down and turned to slither into the garage. And suddenly I could move again. I wanted to get the snake and put it away in its cage and I raced down the steps past Qadira. I entered the garage just in time to see the last of the Cobra's tail disappear underneath our old green couch. When I moved the couch to get to the Cobra I was shocked to discover all these piles of petrified shit.

I woke up that morning trying to understand what the dream meant. It had somehow given me solace. I had to believe that things happen for a reason if I wanted to keep breathing. The meaning of the dream would be revealed to me in due time. Right now it was my job to help Qadira.

Renee busied himself looking up the law. He needed a way to cope and he had learned a thing or two from filing his lawsuit against Nike. He was looking for anything to help Qadira. It was obvious that the jury got this whole thing wrong. Aimee was negligent. How could she not be? And what about Todd? He said he boiled up the water and handed it to her. What the hell? Renee found something called a "judgment notwithstanding the verdict." It was something that could be filed in cases where there was a clear error. Well that was definitely this case. Obviously there was clear error in this case. We tried talking to Scott but suddenly he didn't seem to want to do anything to help Qadira. He was refusing to help. He said he was unwilling to file anything more on behalf of Qadira. He was walking away leaving us to pick up the shattered pieces of our lives.

He came over to our house to try to talk us out of doing anything more. His attitude was something like "you win some you lose some" as if we were just supposed to stand by and let these people get away with this. He wasn't happy to hear that we had called the police. It was a tense meeting that day. I don't remember the details of the conversation but I do remember running outside after Scott as he was leaving. Maybe I just wanted to say one more thing.

But Scott turned towards me and stepped right up in to my face and said "You need to button it down and walk away." I was like did that just happen? Did this white boy just get up in my face, in my neighborhood, and tell me to button it down and walk away? What the fuck was Scott talking about? I thought he was supposed to be helping us? I thought he cared what happened to Qadira. But here he was in my face threatening me? My life just kept getting more and more surreal. SLAP, KICK, PUNCH! They beat us so badly we could barely breathe. My brain never had a minute to process anything but things just kept happening.

I filed a bar complaint on Scott. In our minds he was either completely incompetent or criminally negligent. Obviously his Harvard degree hadn't gotten him much. Either way something didn't smell right. Renee went down to his office and demanded all of our files. Scott hid like a baby in the back room. Renee told the lady at the front desk he would call the police if he didn't get what he came for. The whole circumstance had been infuriating and we wanted some answers. We needed to see what was in Scott's files.

We went down to the courthouse and pulled Qadira's case file trying to determine what evidence had gone back to the jury. Everything was so confusing and imagine our dismay when we discovered Odyssey Program materials printed off the Portland Public Schools website. What the hell was this information doing in her file marked as evidence? Is this what the jurors had been looking at? What did where Qadira went to school have to do with anything? This was getting weirder and weirder.

In fact we now began to think we were now in the Twilight Zone. I found the verdict form and on it the name of the head juror. Her name was Susan Glosser; imagine my surprise when with a stroke of the keyboard I was able to Google this woman. She was some kind of professor up at Lewis and Clark College and she had written a book called Chinese visions of family and state. Anyway turns out she also ran a business out of her house called Opal Mogus Books so she was easy to find and I decided to pay her a visit.

I grabbed the court file, pictures of Qadira's burn injury and headed over the Sellwood Bridge to 8324 SE 16th Ave. I knocked on the door but there was no answer. I heard voices in the backyard and as I called out "hello" a small thin blond girl about Qadira's age appeared from behind the gate. This woman has kids? I was so confused. What had gone back to the jury to make them deem Aimee not negligent? Why were they laughing when they came out of the jury room? The little girl said she would go get her mom so I circled back to the front door and waited.

Susan opened the door just a small crack and peered out at me. She seemed extremely angry and frightened. I opened my folder to the pictures of Qadira's burn and I asked her. "Did you ever see these?" She glanced down at the photos and angrily replied that she had. Then she said I was crazy and that Todd and Aimee had done nothing wrong. She yelled "they paid all of her medical bills." What was she talking about? It was true that State Farm had reimbursed us around 1100 dollars for the medical supplies we had brought at the medical store but the jury had not been privy to that information. That was actually one of the things we had been instructed not to talk about at the trial. Scott said that any mention of insurance would be cause for a mistrial so why was Susan saying this and why was she so mad at me?

She told me to leave and slammed the door in my face. I walked slowly down the stairs and when I reached the sidewalk I froze. I just stood there and started crying. Susan's husband came out of the house and told me if I didn't leave they were going to call the police. He reiterated Susan's stance that Todd and Aimee were not liable for burning up Qadira. He told me that was just the way the law worked. SLAP, KICK, PUNCH! I just couldn't understand these people. But despite the tears I was able to hold my head up high and walk away. I didn't believe a word both of them had told me, and I was going to get to the bottom of this with or without their help.

When I got home I contacted Sergeant Dan Liu who was head of the Child abuse team for the Portland Police. I explained what had happened but Dan Liu didn't seem to care. He wouldn't even take an official report. He kept focusing on the fact that we had lost the trial. He said if we had contacted them before the trial that they would have done an investigation but that a jury verdict was final. But I wasn't buying what he was selling and the conversation got more and more heated. Dan Liu stated loudly that the Portland Police "Do not investigate this type of thing!" and in a final show of contempt he hung up on me. SLAP, KICK, PUNCH! I just couldn't believe it. It was like the whole world had just turned itself inside out. What the hell was going on?

When the weekend rolled around Renee took Qadira down to the police station where an officer Herbert Miller finally took a report. I guess it wasn't so easy to act like a bunch of ass clowns in front of a 9 year old child because we did at least manage to get that pushed through. A few days later we were visited by Firdousi Chowdhury with Child Protective Services coming to inquire after they received the police report. The worker interviewed Qadira about what happened to her and asked to see her scar. It was at this interview that Qadira divulged that Sophie told her that she had been burned playing that game before. It was something I had never heard before and once again I felt caught off guard. The worker said she was going to look into it and I felt relieved that finally somebody would be looking into this. Surely she would be visiting Todd and Aimee's house and then maybe they would have to produce some real answers. But we never heard back from CPS.

Scott withdrew as Qadira's attorney of record and we went back to Stephen P. Riedlinger who agreed to file a motion for a new trial but Judge McShane wasn't having any of it. He was red faced and angry when we appeared in his courtroom and he glared at me with pure hate in his eyes. He showed an obvious contempt for my mother and my friends Bahia and Sean who had the courage to join us in the courtroom. I couldn't understand why he was so angry with me and neither could they. It was very intimidating indeed. What did I do to make this man hate me so much? This wasn't a process, it was a tribunal. I was just trying to obtain some sort of justice for my daughter and here this judge was acting like I was doing something I shouldn't be doing.

Obviously something had gone terribly wrong during the trial and I was just trying to fix it but that was clearly not his perception of the matter. SLAP, KICK, PUNCH! The motion was quickly denied and Riedlinger had done all he was willing to do. Our only other option was filing an appeal but that was going to cost a lot of money we didn't have. Riedlinger did offer to file the notice of appeal but that alone was going to cost over 400 dollars. Then we would have to find an appellate attorney to actually take the case and write the brief. Everything was so confusing. We had to find a way. We couldn't just give up on our daughter.

We met with Robin Morrison who was the principal at Hayhurst to express our growing concern about the improper use of the Odyssey Program materials at the trial. I mean what had Todd and Aimee been trying to imply with this shit anyway? What, like the Native Americans ran around on the prairie naked and that is why they had been doing what they were doing? That is some sick shit if you ask me. She seemed nervous to be talking with us and said that we would have to make an appointment to come back so that a representative of the School district could be present for the conversation.

A couple of weeks later we met with the representative from Portland Public Schools and showed them the Odyssey program materials that we found in Qadira's file but nobody seemed sorry at all. They claimed that the school didn't authorize the use of the materials but in the same breath we were told that if that made us uncomfortable then Qadira was welcome to leave the Odyssey Program. Todd, Aimee, and Sophie weren't going anywhere.

The school district condoned the whole thing. SLAP, KICK,

PUNCH! Shock after shock. Despite what they had done the school was still going to let them volunteer around the children and retain their position in the program. At this point we didn't want Qadira or any of our kids anywhere near these people. This was so fucking insane! In our opinion they had said some very concerning things at the trial and we felt a police investigation of the matter was warranted.

We informed the school that our children were to have no contact with these people and we pulled Qadira out of the Odyssey program. Our only option was to place her into the regular school program on the other side of the school. But it was still stressful because we were still running into Todd, Aimee, and Sophie up at the school, not to mention we couldn't understand the districts reaction. But we had to send our daughter to school and it's not like we had a whole lot of choices. Kymani was still stuck in the Odyssey Program for another year due to the stupid lottery process. We were stuck for now. We had no idea how to proceed. Periodically I would also see the old woman who sat on the jury picking up her grand kids. Boy did I feel like getting a gun and mowing a few people down. It was hard to sleep at night listening to the blood boil in my veins.

I heard tales of Todd boasting all over the neighborhood how they had "won" the trial. The sideways looks from the neighbors were everywhere. There seemed to be this consensus that we were in the wrong for suing Todd and Aimee. Never mind that Scott was the attorney and we had only done what he had suggested.

It was like someone playing naked games with your kid and burning them with a teakettle was just normal everyday stuff. To them Qadira was just some toy that Sophie broke. As usual race was factor that could not be ignored. Our daughter couldn't be just a little Human Being who had suffered a terrible injury at the hands of an irresponsible adult. Someone always had to be more valuable than someone else. Everyone around us associated color with race. It was absolute insanity! In our new cruel world she was one little brown child who didn't carry a monetary designation worth protecting. It was so terrible. It was Todd and Aimee that seemed to garner all the sympathy.

Poor Todd and Aimee. Everyone seemed to feel so sorry for them because they burned up Qadira? What the hell was going on? One neighbor said to my face that once her kid fell out of a tree at someone's house and got a little cut on his leg but they didn't sue anybody. This wasn't a little cut you stupid fucking bitch, I thought to myself while maintaining a forced smile on my face. There was no comparison so I don't know why she tried to make one. Why would you sue somebody because your kid fell out of a tree especially if they were not hurt? What the fuck was she implying? She said her son hadn't even needed to go to the hospital or anything like that so what the fuck?

Qadira's burn injury had needed a little more attention than some Neosporin and a Band-Aid. What the fuck? Qadira had been seriously injured by scalding water and scarred for life but suddenly it was all fun and games? I was standing there wanting to reach out and slap this woman's face but I held my composure. How dare she compare some little cut her son got to my daughter being burned up by a teakettle? These people were making me sick to my stomach! Although they may not want to admit it now I am 100 percent sure if we had burned up little white Sophie the neighbors would have gotten out their pitchforks and knives and Renee and I would have been placed under the jail.

And our problems were growing larger by the minute because we were completely out of money and credit. You can't live on this planet without money and we were getting this lesson hard and fast. It hadn't taken very long before Renee was fired from his welding job at Gunderson. He had made the mistake of mentioning that he had a small pain in his back and his supervisor had sent him to the nurse who then sent him to a doctor where the fact that he had injured his back in a car accident some years ago caused a problem.

He hadn't mentioned the accident on his initial application because he was afraid they wouldn't hire him if he did and we were desperate. The company considered this a "misrepresentation" since he was supposed to have disclosed something like that on the application and boom! So great now Renee was out of work again. I had already been forced to take a break from my job at Benchview due to all the stress I was under. My mom and sister had already hired someone else so now we were without any income at all.

And so it happened that just days after losing the trial we were on our way down to the welfare office to apply for food and cash. SLAP, KICK, PUNCH! More stress to add to the stress. It seemed silly that Renee and I would be applying for benefits simply because

Nike had a hair up its ass and decided to obliterate Renee's prospects for some kind of job in his industry but here we were. It's not like there was a lack of footwear design or color design jobs to be had but for Renee there was nothing.

From one horrible situation to the next we had to keep going for our kids. Now our plump worker was talking to us about the mafia and how "they" could watch everything that you were doing. She seemed to be implying something but we couldn't figure out what? She sounded insane. The world had turned into some kind of freak show and after the trial I didn't even know what to believe anymore. We weren't going to ask what she meant because it was too difficult to believe the words coming out of her mouth. We just wanted to get out of there as fast as possible. It was just the beginning of multiple encounters with people in positions of authority that would fail to make any sense.

We listened to her stories and nodded our heads and smiled in all the appropriate places. Luckily somehow they would take care of our mortgage payment for the next month giving Renee and I a little bit of time to find some kind of work before we were in serious danger of losing our house. It wasn't much of a reprieve but it was something. A few months prior to Qadira's trial as we watched our meager savings dwindle we had put the house up for sale in hopes of being able to downsize and get a little money to secure some kind of future but in the downed economy nobody was biting. The house still needed too much work for the kind of buyers we were encountering.

And in order to keep our welfare benefits we were forced to go to these job training classes in a dirty little room full of downtrodden and depressed people. Even the people that worked there looked ready to jump off the next bridge they could find. We had to put together these resumes and look for work which was of course another huge slap in the face for Renee. He was beaten until he couldn't breathe. SLAP, KICK, PUNCH! It was extra especially hard for him because employers were always suspicious. Why would a Nike designer apply for a minimum wage job? When Renee explained to the welfare worker, who was teaching the class, that he couldn't get a job because he was being discriminated against; nobody cared. He was just supposed to go through the motions.

It was heartbreaking to watch him apply for job after job in the footwear industry and get no response. Everyone he knew turned their backs on him hard. It was really ugly. And it was painfully apparent that the welfare system isn't designed to really help anyone. As a matter of fact they make you feel like a piece of human waste. There was a girl in our class who said her dream was to work with children and she talked about wanting to open up her own daycare but the welfare workers weren't there to encourage anybody.

This wasn't a place set up to help people get self-sufficient. Most of the DHS workers were just a bunch of overweight, underpaid, tired, depressed, and stressed out individuals toiling away for a paycheck that barely provided the means to exist. They might as well have just posted a sign on the front door that said "Find a minimum wage job or go kill yourself." There is nothing like a trip down to the local welfare office to make you feel completely worthless.

And the police were refusing to investigate the whole thing and I found myself calling and writing all of my elected officials who just kept telling me there was nothing they could do without a police investigation. SLAP, KICK, PUNCH! I just couldn't accept their response because it made no sense. They refused to directly address any of my concerns or explain in any type of coherent manner what had occurred at the trial. I was just supposed to believe that it was somehow okay for these people to have burned up my child and not have taken any responsibility? It was just too hard to believe. Aimee wasn't negligent at all? How? How was this even possible? I knew the system was bad but surely it wasn't this bad?

I needed to know what was in those depositions and because of my official appointment as "guardian ad litem" I was going to be able to order them up. I was embarking on an unexpected journey with a destination unknown to me. I set out to find the truth. It was around this time I was reminded about the dream I had of Qadira and the cobra. My cousin was getting married and I ended up attending her wedding in Wisconsin. I was surprised when I stepped into my aunt's house to find cobras everywhere reinforcing my dream. Statues and paintings. I knew the dream meant something. I knew I had to keep going.

I didn't know what to expect when I ordered the depositions of Todd, Aimee, Sophie, and Renee but I had to know what was in them. And when they appeared in the mail I ended up getting the shock of my life. SLAP, KICK, PUNCH! I could hardly make sense of what I was now faced with. Aimee's deposition was the thinnest one of the bunch while Renee's was obviously the largest. I decided to start with Aimee's. What on earth could Scott have been asking her I wondered?

I settled down in my room to read. One of the first questions Scott asked her was "What is your husband's name?" To which Aimee replied Todd Burkholder. And then Scott asked "is that any relation to Rex?" To which Aimee replied "yes brothers." But who was Rex Burkholder? I had never heard of anybody named Rex Burkholder. What did he have to do with anything?

I went to do a Google search and my stomach nearly dropped out of my ass. Suddenly I felt like I was gasping for breath. A politician? Todd's brother was a Portland Metro Councilor. Some long time politician with all kinds of connections all over the place. The more I read the more I learned. If there was a hell then I was in it. Scott hadn't been acting as Qadira's attorney. He had clearly been working for the other side. What the fuck?! The depositions were so bizarre. Scott questioning Todd, Aimee, and Sophie about our family? Asking them if any one of them had ever seen us mad? Asking Todd about my mom's behavior the night of the burn?

And then Todd talking mad shit about my mom saying she didn't care about Qadira? Scott asking Todd what the inside of our house looked like? Scott asking Todd what Todd's impressions of our family were? Todd saying he thought we just wanted some money! That he didn't think we cared about our daughter or the fact she was burned! OMG!!! Asking Aimee if she had ever seen Qadira wearing short skirts?

Todd talking about how they were playing "Little house on the prairie." Sophie and Todd talking about how Qadira had bathed over there once before but Aimee saying she wasn't sure if she had or not. SLAP, KICK, PUNCH! It was insanity! Scott hadn't been honest with us at all. He and Rudy had put me and my family on a train and taken us for a ride. I was so sick, Sick, SICK!! I was starting to understand why I couldn't get any help. It was a massive blow to the gut and I was so fucking sick and tired of the bullshit!! I could feel the steam seeping out of my ears. This motherfucker was not going to get away with this shit!

I was absolutely livid about the entire circumstance and on October 13th 2008 I sent a very comprehensive letter to the Chief of the Portland Police Rosie Sizer requesting an investigation alleging that Scott Kocher and Rudy Lachenmeier had conspired to cover up a crime. I was actively looking for a way around the brick wall I kept running into. Renee had trouble stomaching the details. In my letter I detailed everything that had happened at and leading up to the trial but the chief of police didn't even bother to respond.

It was just blow after blow after blow. SLAP, KICK, PUNCH! If I had the choice to die I would have picked death. The pain was too much. My whole world was different and it was a "learn as you go" situation. We were getting a crash course in "There is no system for you" and it hurt like hell! And On October 29th 2008 out of the blue Phil Knight did something completely out of character. He suddenly gave OHSU 100 million dollars. Many in the media speculated as to why. At the time we didn't even notice.

STEPHENS VS. NIKE

We were in a pressure cooker. Our mailbox was overflowing with legal papers and suddenly Renee was getting calls from Stoel Rives. That's right; Nike had hired the largest law firm on the West Coast to defend against the lawsuit. SLAP, KICK, PUNCH! Amy Joseph Pederson and P.K. Runkles Pearson were about to take center stage in our life. Our everyday normal had turned into a Lifetime original movie. I never knew what to expect from day to day. We had both landed jobs as security guards with ABM and we were fighting to keep our heads above water on a sinking ship. Our mortgage of nearly 1800.00 a month was threatening to totally break us. The house just was not selling and we would have given anything to get the hell out of this place.

The universe was clearly telling us no again. We were so world weary that waking up had turned into a chore. When I wasn't at work or taking care of the kids I was drinking away my sorrows so I could get out of my own head. The pressure was so intense that sometimes I had to talk myself into bothering to breath. It was pure torture of the worst kind. My friends quickly began to fade away and eventually we found ourselves all alone in a deep dark tunnel. I no longer had the nice life with the husband that worked at Nike so why would anyone really want to know me? Our situation made us lepers in our community. We didn't have a normal anymore. I didn't want a bunch of fair weather friends anyway. Only Haley kept coming around.

We were learning to live in the moment, just to be glad to get through the next minute. My feet felt like too big lead bricks but I just tried to keep moving forward. We would get up in the morning and shower and get dressed. Take the kids to school, go to work, make dinner, study the law, yell at a police officer, study the law, get the kids off to school, study the law, and then get up the next day and do it all over again. The mornings were bittersweet as we awoke in the same nightmare over and over again. It was like "Oh my God this is really our life?"

The brightest lights that we could see shone out from our children and we tried to follow them. They were a constant reminder that there was still something right with the world. They guided us. For them we tried to keep putting on the best show we could. Failure wasn't an option. It wasn't always pleasant but we were together. We were alive. We laughed, we cried, we tried as hard as we could not to give up.

We remained hopeful that somehow and someway, things would work out. We operated on a belief that we just needed to elevate our situation to the right person. Certainly not every single person that we encountered could be corrupt could they? But we were quickly learning that such is the power of the almighty dollar. We wrote all of our elected officials over and over explaining our situation and one by one they wrote us back to say there was nothing they could do.

And then one day on the way to Qadira's counseling appointment we ended up face to face with Aimee at a stop sign. She was in her car and we were in ours just one block from our house. We had just picked Qadira up from school so she was seated in the back seat of the van. We hadn't seen her since the trial and we all stared at her in disbelief. For a moment time froze and we froze with it. Suddenly Aimee's face turned bright red and she poked her tongue out at us as if to say "nah, nah, nah, nah, nah, nah, you can't get me." I felt my hand on the door handle and I heard the click as the door popped open.

I was going to wipe the pavement with this bitches head! No she did not just stick her tongue out at me!! This bitch was going to burn my daughter up with a teakettle and just walk away!?

I imagined slamming her head into the pavement over and over as her brains spilled all over the concrete. I swung my legs out the door but suddenly I couldn't move. Renee had grabbed my sweater and was pulling me back. This wasn't the way he said. I was so heated for a second I tried to fight him off so I could get to where I wanted to go. My heart was beating loudly in my ears and every breath going in and out was filled with pain. Then I could hear my daughter telling me to calm down. I realized that my daughter was in the car and suddenly reality came back into focus. I was listening to Qadira's voice "Mom" she yelled "CALM DOWN!" She was frantic. I took a deep breath and closed the door.

Renee and Qadira were right it probably wasn't the best idea to kick Aimee's ass but it sure would have felt good. And if I couldn't just go beat up Aimee then I sure as hell was going to speak up and speak out about what had happened. I made it my mission to elevate what had happened to Qadira whenever I could. There wasn't an official in Portland who didn't receive some type of notice of what had happened to Qadira. Over and over we appealed for help and doors were slammed in our faces repeatedly. SLAP, KICK, PUNCH.

We started turning over every rock we could to find Qadira an appellate attorney. We reasoned that if we could just put Qadira's case in front of the Appellate Court the judges would see the light and surely the case would be remanded and our nightmare would end. There was a way a right way to get justice for our daughter. This wasn't her fault. She was a child. Come hell or high water these people would be held accountable for what they had done.

But by this time I also had to help Renee prepare for depositions. It was an intense juggling act that required a whole lot of time and effort that we really didn't have. We hardly ever slept anymore. It wasn't uncommon for us to stay up for days on end. There were days when I would fall asleep at the wheel and wake up just in time to avert a major disaster.

There was so much work to do all of the time. Renee's deposition was approaching fast and the pressure cooker was turned all the way up to high. People go to school for years to become attorneys and we were taking a crash course all by ourselves preparing to fight a giant. And to make matters worse, all of the appellate attorney's we talked to about Qadira's case kept saying "no." In the midst of all that stress we were preparing to send Renee into the lion's den.

The world was spinning out of control and we just kept going through the motions. More and more we were drinking in order to dull the pain. Everything just kind of hurt all of the time and there was no reaching out to anyone for support. Nobody seemed to understand no matter how hard we tried to explain it. Nobody would help us.

Renee did his best to keep talking to attorneys and they kept saying no. Sometimes we would wish so hard for an attorney but after what Scott had done we weren't sure if we wanted our wishes to come true. We were just going to have to go into this thing with a hope and a belief of better things to come. We had to believe that the judge would see that Nike was wrong. After all, the EEOC had left us with 3 indeterminate findings. There was a chance.

After all how could any of this possibly be permanent? We needed answers. Some type of resolution. I was hot under the collar contacting every official that I could think of to get some help for Qadira. We decided to go back to Stephen P. Reidlinger and asked him to go ahead and file the notice of appeal. He had said he would at least help us do that after the motion for a new trial failed. But he also warned us that he would not be willing to write the brief. We dug down deep into our pockets to make it happen. It was our only chance.

We figured since the actual opening brief didn't need to be filed for several months we still had plenty of time to find an attorney to write the thing. Sure the prospects looked pretty bleak considering what had happened at the trial but Qadira was a child, surely somebody would agree to help us. We vowed to leave no stone unturned. It was difficult to accept that the system was completely broken because it was the only system we had.

Surely there had to be some type of reasonable way to right this wrong. And so on November 12th of 2008 Qadira's notice of appeal was filed extending our chances to seek justice for our daughter. The fight wasn't over yet giving us some kind of hope for the future. This must have sent a shock out across the legal community because it was on the same day that my husband was subjected to a rather lengthy deposition by one P.K Runkles Pearson and Amy Joseph Pederson of Stoel Rives. Nike wanted to know everything and they wanted the whole encounter on video tape.

When we arrived at Stoel Rives on the morning of November the 12th we were both extremely nervous and scared not knowing what to expect. We were led back to a very expensive conference room and asked to wait. The room reminded me of the some of the rooms I had sat in when Scott had pretended to represent Qadira. Were these attorneys as shady as Scott Kocher? At first we were worried that they were going to ask me to leave. They came in looking super official and educated. I felt small and inadequate in my discount Target dress pants and hand me down blouse. I was sweating and my cheap lipstick and Payless shoes suddenly seemed to be sticking out like a big red sore thumb. "Oh my God" I thought to myself "What on Earth were we doing here?"

There was no way I was going to leave Renee all alone without any support but I certainly didn't belong here. At least my husband had dressed well for the occasion in the only suit he owned. It was the same suit we had brought for him to wear to his father's funeral just last year. P.K Runkles Pearson and Amy Joseph Pederson were displeased with my presence but agreed to let me stay. Their lack of empathy for the situation was apparent.

This wasn't about right or wrong. This was war and they were out for blood. SLAP, KICK, PUNCH! The deposition lasted 2 whole days and I watched the whole thing. They asked my husband everything, anything, and all those things in between. They left no stone unturned, but his story was always the same. The funny thing about the truth is it's easy to prove and even easier to remember.

I thought to myself that P.K was a strange looking woman. She looked to be in her late 30's or early 40's but her hair was all grey. Like a bitter old lady had stolen what was left of her youth. Her voice was robotic and she was methodical in her approach. She asked question after question. At times Renee appeared drained and utterly exhausted but somehow he managed to keep himself together. He was as he always was. More polite, cordial and kind than most people would have been able to be considering the situation. But of course for those of you who are really curious there is a video of the whole thing.

And things didn't stop there because the next day I received a letter from the Oregon Department of Justice claiming that they had no authority to force the Portland Police to do an investigation into what had happened to Qadira. I thought my head was going to explode! So all the police had to do was refuse to investigate and that was it?

And then a few days later on the 17th another SLAP in the face as the Oregon State Bar dismissed my complaint against Scott Kocher claiming that he had done nothing wrong because he had gone to "Harvard." That was not any kind of explanation. They slapped us and beat us with impunity. So people who go to Harvard don't commit crimes? It was like what the fucking fuck!!!! I immediately appealed the decision stating among other things that "I did not believe that a Harvard education was an indication that someone was ethical or trustworthy." And then it was the waiting game again. What in the world was wrong with these people?

December came and once again we were faced with another Christmas. This was one holiday that I wished we could postpone. It was very hard to get into it but we put the tree up and counted our blessings. Last year had been terrible and now 2009 wasn't looking any better. My nerves were totally shot. Not only had we felt the wrath of the Shoe Giant at Renee's deposition, he was now preparing to do his very own depositions.

Stoel Rives had so graciously agreed to let him use one of their conference rooms and we had hired none other than Bridge City Legal to do the job. This was costing us a whole lot of money we did not have. We had taken a big risk and stopped paying our mortgage in order to keep up the fight. And on December 17th Renee was just going to go ahead and depose the CEO of Exeter Brands Group, Claire Hamill herself. The stress we were under was unreal.

Claire had been well apprised of Renee's complaint and she along with Mary and Mac had been the ones who had taken it upon themselves to fire Renee a year and a half ago. Claire and Randy were friends and it was possible that Claire had chosen to retaliate against Renee for complaining. It was no secret that Claire was a homosexual so it was possible that she may have perceived Renee's complaint as an insult to her way of life. We had reasoned by making the claim of sex discrimination that if Renee had been a female the company would take a different approach. Certainly we believed that they would not have referred to what had occurred as "roughhousing."

Claire who had only been named President and CEO of Exeter Brands Group in January of 2007 just weeks before Renee complained had many interesting answers to Renee's questions that day. She claimed that she hadn't been appointed President and CEO to shut the company down, yet that is apparently exactly what she chose to set into motion behind closed doors in April of 2007, just weeks after Renee complained. Despite the protection of Nike's high priced attorneys Claire was all over the map when confronted with Renee himself. He met her on the battlefield with no shield but the truth. His composure never faulted and Nike found themselves face to face with a formidable adversary.

The very next day on December 18th he was preparing to come face to face with Cory and Mary. He was most nervous to see Cory and once again I debated my presence at the function. Once again we decided that Renee should go this one alone. He wanted me to come with him but we weren't 100 percent sure of anything and Renee didn't want to further embarrass Cory. We both thought it would be best if he faced Cory by himself. What had happened had been horrible and humiliating and the last thing he wanted to be doing was talking about it to anybody.

It was safe to assume that Cory felt the same way. And as it turned out we were right. Cory didn't look so good that day and what he had to say was even worse. At the time of the incident Cory had been under a massive amount of stress due to a multitude of family issues. He had been trying to leave Nike to be closer his mother who was alone in California after his father died, his wife's brother had been shot and killed and then of course Randy had assaulted him. Of course Cory has maintained that he does not remember because who would want to remember any of that? News flash people, people who have jobs also have lives so that's just something we should all be mindful of here. I am sure the last thing Cory needed was Randy jumping on him.

And then of course there was Mary. Blond, privileged, high school graduate, completely unqualified to be assessing victims of sexual assault, talking all kinds of nonsense trying to nervously bumble her way through Renee's questions. What a circus this was turning out to be. When asked how she would have felt if someone had tried to "dry-hump" her on the job, Mary replied "shocked and appalled." Why Nike was defending this behavior and putting all these people through all of this we still do not know?

It was so simple, so cut and dry, but there were even worse things happening in the background that we were not privy to; terrible things. People were angry. Businesses had been put in peril and money had been lost. Every day we kept our heads above water, every day that we got up, got dressed, and faced another day Nike was losing money. Here we were just trying to access our rights so we could survive and in the midst of all that they were throwing every weapon they could at us. It was a brutal bloody battle and we were losing badly.

Around this time we were still holding out hope on the complaint that I had filed against Judge McShane for willful misconduct but we were dismayed once again to get a dismissal without explanation the day after Christmas. There didn't seem to be anyway to fix what had happened and I was spiraling deeper and deeper down into depression every day. If I wasn't taking care of the kids or working then I was drinking. There was Rolling Rock in the fridge and Evan Williams in the cupboard. I was in physical distress from dealing with everything that had happened. My 10 dollar an hour job as a security guard with ABM Security couldn't be much worse. My body was literally on fire from all of the stress and there wasn't any end in sight.

I don't know how we made it through the holidays that year. We just went through the motions because we didn't know what else to do and we were still here. We didn't even care about the holidays anymore but we just had to do something for the kids. They wouldn't understand if we just gave up. They were counting on us. What would we tell them if everything just fell apart? We couldn't expect them to understand all of this and they obviously expected us to take care of them.

We were grateful that they had each other because it felt like a real job to stay present. We continued trying in the only way we knew how to keep them somewhat sheltered from the dark cloud that had settled over our lives. On my darkest nights I would think to myself how much I didn't want to wake up in the morning. But then the morning would come anyway to slap me in the face. It was like a recurring nightmare that had no end in sight.

And then January 7th 2009 rolled around. Another cold winter day and another round of depositions with Nike but this time I wasn't about to let Renee go into the belly of the beast all by himself again. This time he would be facing off with Randy. I was nervous as hell but come hell or high water we were determined to go in together. If Nike could have their fancy cameras' and high priced lawyers then certainly Renee could have me there. He couldn't keep going in alone. Runkles tried to make an issue of it but Renee had done his research and the truth is anyone can attend a deposition. I wasn't budging and Runkles didn't like it. Even in a depressed state of mind my attitude was hard at work making the people around me, despite their credentials, extremely irritated.   After all who was I to just park myself in the middle of their party?

Randy came in looking like the cat that ate the canary and I just wanted to smack the shit out of him. He looked guilty but he certainly wasn't sorry. He had his "white privilege" to protect him, and if that wasn't enough, he had Nike's attorneys available to coddle him if Renee's question's caused him too much distress. Everything to this guy was just one big joke. And why shouldn't it be? Why should someone who's not facing any consequences care how they conduct themselves?

After all, look what he had gotten away with, and here was the company hiring up all these big time attorneys just to defend him. So naturally he just sat there and ran his mouth. If Cory couldn't remember then Randy would remember for the both of them. And just when I thought things couldn't get any more bizarre we found ourselves in another out of this world situation. During Randy's deposition we had decided to all take a break.

Renee as usual had brought along his little voice recorder so he could have audio of the depositions. While he was away in the bathroom I had heard a loud argument in the conference room. I imagined that the lawyers were angry with Randy for sitting there and basically admitting to the whole thing. Unfortunately I wasn't able to make out any actual words from my position on the bench but my imagination couldn't have been too far off the mark.

When we re-entered the room Runkles had a bone to pick with that recorder. Apparently Renee had forgotten to turn the thing off so whatever they had all been arguing about had been caught on tape. Runkles was furious and asked Renee to give her the recorder so she could erase what had presumably been caught on tape. But the company had agreed to allow Renee to have the recorder and why should we just go along with what she was asking? Renee was in the process of trying to figure out what action if any we should take when suddenly Runkles jumped across the conference table with a wild look in her eye and attempted to snatch the recorder from Renee's hands.

Time was in slow motion as I watched the struggle for a moment. It was certainly unexpected behavior from someone of P.K's standing. Important high priced attorneys didn't behave like this. If Renee had wanted to he could have overpowered the woman but he was a gentleman at heart and when he realized what was happening he let go of the machine in favor of retaining his dignity. The poor court reporter was trying to contain her shock as I loudly suggested that we go ahead and call the police. The situation was very intimidating and Renee decided that he didn't want to inflame an already tense situation. Someone from the tech department at Stoel Rives was called up to oversee erasing all of the disputed information. I have often wondered what was on that tape, but I guess only Randy, Runkles, and Pederson will ever really know.

Then Mac and Melissa had their say. Like each individual who was called to the table suddenly their "little joke" of ruining Renee's life didn't seem so funny. There was an intense energy radiating from Renee's dark eyes and he gave each person who sat before him a soul stare that was hard to ignore. They struggled to find the right words to defend their actions all those months ago. It was crystal clear like all spoiled brats that they had never ever anticipated having to explain themselves. They had conducted the whole thing like a college hazing with no regard for the outcome or anyone's feelings and now they had to sit across from their victim and pretend to be okay with themselves. It wasn't going so well.

And then I was called to the table to speak on Renee's behalf. Runkles tried to come at me hard but I stood my ground. Again she took advantage of me because she could and like in Renee's deposition they asked me all sorts of thing that would have never been allowed had I had an attorney present. But of course the legal community had been put on notice and we weren't going to be getting any kind of help or protection. Nike was digging for any dirt that they could find. She was looking hard for discord in our marriage and anything else they could find to tear us down. It was open season on the Stephens. But of course there was really nothing to tell. They basically obtained nothing from these interchanges that they already didn't know. Before Renee had complained at Nike we had just been regular people doing regular things.

January 9th 2009 the depositions were finished after Renee briefly questioned Allison Daugherty who was another person in HR that had handled some aspects of his complaint. It was same old same old as the Nike employees were totally unsure of how to conduct themselves in this situation. More information continued to be spilled in our favor. The case was cut and dry and we were beginning to gain some confidence that we could actually win this thing and get our life back. Settlement conferences were being set up for January 30th 2009 and we anticipated the closing of this terrible chapter in our lives. The depositions had been a success. Now that Randy and the others had admitted to what they had done on paper maybe finally some sort of justice would be served. The stress was killing me and I chopped off my nearly waist long hair straight up to my ears. It was too much.

Things with Qadira seemed to have gotten a little better. The weekly counseling seemed to be helping. It certainly gave me some piece of mind. After the trial we had worried so much about what had really happened that night. Qadira had been severely injured and traumatized the night of the burn and due to all the lies we had encountered we tried to make sure that there were not going to be any more surprises. I figured if there were any dark repressed memories they would surface and we could confront them. Todd and Aimee had been so dishonest, Scott and Rudy had lied, and we were ever more grateful despite the adverse outcome that we had not brought Qadira to the trial.

We found ourselves trying to be grateful for the smallest of things. We held steadfastly to the hope that this would all be over soon. Maybe, just maybe Nike would loosen its grip on us and we could resume our lives to some degree. I imagined Renee getting his job back in the footwear industry. One time on a response to one of their emails we attached pictures of our kids in hopes that they would end the siege. It would have been so nice to not have to be struggling so hard to survive. Maybe I would be able to quit my horribly difficult job and go back to school. With great anticipation we awaited the settlement conferences and before we knew it we were headed to the Washington County courthouse for the big day.

We had no idea what was in store for us but P.K Runkles Pearson and Amy Joseph Pederson were sure being nice to me. "Oh Karellen" they exclaimed "You cut your hair." I wasn't sure what to make of their sugary sweet demeanor because I was pretty sure these ladies didn't like me. And then out stepped Judge Mark Gardener.

He was a slightly chubby old man with a jovial disposition and as the day wore on it became increasingly clear that he couldn't stomach the situation.

Nike wanted to settle the whole thing for 40,000 dollars and they just wouldn't budge. I wasn't having any of it because just the debt alone that we had incurred as a result of all this amounted to that much, not to mention the loss of Renee's retirement fund and the fact that he was blacklisted. I didn't see what we could really get done with the 40,000 dollars? Sure we could pay off our credit card debt but Renee needed a job. We had a house and a mortgage that we could barely pay for and 4 kids in tow that needed all kinds of things that we needed to provide for. Renee had had an up and coming career before all of this and he had done nothing wrong. Why couldn't he just have his job back?

The frustration amongst the attorneys and the Nike representative Erin Potempa was mounting. They kept leaving the room to go talk among themselves and towards the end of the day along with the 40,000 they offered Renee a letter of recommendation that he could supposedly use to get another job. Renee was tired and ready to give up. We went out in the hall to talk. I believed in my husband and I told him to stand his ground. At this point I was totally fed up with the entire process. This wasn't going the way I had imagined at all. Why were they giving my husband such a hard time? The attorneys even had to admit that Renee had been well liked at Nike. So why not give him a job back? Besides he had gotten enough rejection to know for a fact that his name had been slandered in the industry.

There was absolutely no guarantee that their supposed letter of recommendation would do a damn thing to get us out of the poverty we were now being subjected to. We were just supposed to trust that? He had already applied and been rejected from just about everywhere. He had left no stone unturned in his search to find work. If we took the deal we would have no more recourse and the 40,000 dollars wouldn't even be enough the cover the debt we were now swimming in. We dug in. If they wanted him to never work in the industry again they were going to have to pay for that because we needed to be able to get back on our feet. We asked for 100,000 dollars and a job. That was reasonable and a drop in the bucket for Nike. It would be enough to at least recoup what we had lost.

We could put his retirement money back and pay off the debt we had incurred since all this started and resume our life. That was fair. But saying no to Nike's offer and attempting to recoup our losses was like throwing down the gauntlet because the attorneys came in angry after speaking to Judge Gardener. SLAP, KICK, PUNCH! They told my husband to "never apply at their company ever again." Erin Potempa was visibly red faced and shaking with anger when the attorney's announced this next stipulation.

Mark Gardener was also visibly unnerved. He told us in private "I told them to give you a job." He likened to what was happening to an open wound. We were nice people and we didn't deserve what was happening to us and he could see that. He had tried to reason with the Nike attorneys but they had their marching orders from corporate. They were to obliterate Renee. There was to be no mercy after what he had done. In the eyes of the Nike elite we had no right to even exist. But Judge Gardener must have seen the fire in my eyes. He said "I told them that the wife said no." And then he looked directly at me and said "I told them that you said no."

A wise man knows that conviction and faith are powerful weapons indeed. He could see that I believed in my husband. He nervously told us some good things that he remembered about Nike. He talked about how he just wanted to go home and have a beer. His hands were shaking. The man behind the curtain was in over his head and he wanted out. The meeting was to be adjourned. We had the weekend to think about our options which were take the money and walk away or try to keep fighting the enraged giant. Judge Gardener had reluctantly refused to appoint Renee counsel obviously at the bidding of his master, so, if we wanted to move forward we would have to do so, on our own. SLAP, KICK, PUNCH! Things were looking pretty bleak.

The day had turned out to be one big disappointment and the weekend stretching out before us wasn't looking any better. Renee was on the fence about things. He had begun to doubt himself. I was a hot mess but I was clear. We couldn't just let them get away with this. We had lost so much. Moving forward seemed like the only way we could ever get back on our feet. Renee was wasting his life doing security. I felt strongly that he needed to clear his good name and get back to what he did best. He had worked so hard to get into design it just didn't seem fair that he would lose his career over something like this.

It burned me up inside that Randy had been given a promotion to Design Director after Renee complained and was sitting over there at Nike with a raise while we barely had two pennies to rub together. These over-privileged assholes had no idea what it was like for people like us. They were just used to just getting their way all the time. If the shoes were on the other feet most of them would have already checked out. How would Randy or Cory feel if they had their child abused, their life savings taken from them, and been blacklisted from doing the only thing they really knew how to do?

Yes I spent many hours wondering how these people would feel in our situation and I imagined that most of them probably would have killed themselves had they been offered a walk in our shoes. We decided not to take the money. And the very next day to rub salt in the wound I received a letter from Sylvia E. Stevens, General Counsel for the Oregon State Bar officially closing my complaint against Scott Kocher. But we kept telling ourselves that we just hadn't knocked on enough doors. We kept telling ourselves that somehow this injustice would be righted.

We kept breathing, we kept getting up, and we kept taking the kids to school, going to work, making dinner. We got good at going through the motions and then drowning our sorrows in the bottom of every kind of bottle. Being sober was physically painful at this time. I didn't like to be reminded of who I had been, what I was, or who I was becoming. Back then one of our favorite movies was The Prince of Egypt. We watched it over and over. It gave us something to relate to.

This fight had become almost biblical. It was like Renee had been raised in the palace and then kicked out into the wilderness. This fight was bigger than just us. People had fought and died for us to have a right and it wasn't our right to just give up and walk away. On February 17th when Nike filed its awesomely huge motion for summary judgment (oh I am not kidding you should go take a look at the size of that thing!) we brushed away any feeling of intimidation and put our noses to the grindstone. We would do the work God sent us to do.

Now you really won't believe this but Nike had no real arguments. Their position rested solely on their assertion that the Plaintiff (my husband) had "been subjected to a bunch of crude jokes." They didn't bother to deny what happened; they just embraced it full on.

Basically, dry-humping on the Nike campus is just perfectly fine they said. Renee being fired and blacklisted had nothing to do with any of that, no that was all because of the so called Exeter shutdown which they refused to put into evidence. We even suspected that Nike hadn't even really shut Exeter down. Their claim that Exeter was still open but did no business and had no employee's seemed a little far-fetched even to us. Why would Nike have suddenly "pitted" a lucrative business? We came back swinging.

This fight no longer belonged to us. We convinced ourselves that all of this had a much greater purpose. It wasn't "our work" it was "The work" and we did it. We both felt absolutely moved to respond. Every time we had to write another court brief we told ourselves that "The work" had to be done. And putting together a professional response to refute summary judgment wasn't going to be easy. We only had until March 9th to turn something in. Looking back after all these years I am not sure where we got the words or the strength to do anything. Renee was David and Nike was Goliath. We had a bag of rocks and they had a nuclear bomb. We weren't about to give up or give in. The people we were dealing with were monsters but most regular people were good. If we could overcome summary judgment we could put the case in front of a jury and we were pretty positive that the people would see to it that justice was done.

We just needed the judge to do his job. With all the material facts of the case still at issue, all the judge was supposed to do was send the case to trial. We had a right to a trial. Normal people could appreciate Renee's position. Most men that we talked to about this readily announced that if that had happened to them they would have knocked Randy out. Of course that would not have helped Renee at the time because it would have been his word against Randy's and if he had laid even one finger on Randy he would have most certainly been charged with assault on top of being fired. It was long days and even longer nights. We hardly slept anymore. Between caring for the kids, the legal work, and our security jobs we didn't have time for much else, not that there was much else. Our financial situation took care of that.

So on March 9th we filed our response to their motion for summary judgment. By now the paperwork associated with this case filled up several boxes. We were beginning to sink from the strain of all the legal fees. We lowered the price of the house as far down as we could but it just would not sale. The stress was overwhelming.

The something that everyone around us was trying to pretend was nothing was multiplying into a whole lot of everything. We tried to drum up support for our cause by protesting. We made big signs and before and after work we spent the week of Easter that year standing in front of Nike's world headquarters. We placed ourselves right across the street so whenever anyone left campus we could be seen. The sign read "DON'T SPEAK UP YOU'LL LOSE YOUR JOB, NIKE DOESN'T CARE ABOUT WORKER'S RIGHTS."

Renee had worked up at Nike for 8 years and he knew a lot of people. We were creating a stomachache in the belly of the beast and angering our opponent with what they viewed as our disobedience. Who were we? Two little brown people who were worth nothing to be marching around like we mattered? The giant grew angrier by the hour. In the background unbeknownst to us the town was being shut down around us. The media wouldn't cover the case, no attorney would go near it with a ten foot pole, and there was little chance of ending up in front of a judge that didn't work for the money. But we didn't know all of this. We were still operating with a belief that we lived in the United States of America and that somewhere there was a system and a rule of law that said that people mattered.

The night before the hearing Renee became violently ill from the stress. He was having stomach pains so severe that we wound up in the emergency room. I had never seen him like this. His stomach looked like a tight round ball and I was reminded of that old T.V series "V" when a girl birthed an alien baby. The stress was taking its toll. The doctors were saying that it could just be a bad case of constipation so they gave him a bunch of laxatives to clear him out. We sat around in the emergency room for a few hours but nothing was happening. After a couple of hours his stomach calmed down and they released him. It was 6:00 in the morning and we had to be at the hearing at 9:00.

We tried to lie down and close our eyes for a few minutes. It would be terrible to run off the road on the way to the courthouse. Around 8:00 Renee finally felt like something was happening and he made his way to the bathroom to relieve himself. When he finally emerged he said "I feel like I shit my brains out." He looked completely exhausted, but thank goodness that the doctor had been right. Boy was I glad that was over. The last thing we needed was something super serious happening with Renee's health. I certainly wasn't going to make it alone. But there was no time to talk. I had already taken the kids to school so it was time to go. Maybe today finally everything would be all over. We were all very hopeful.

Renee got dressed in the same old suit he had worn to the depositions because that was all he had and I slipped on my Target dress pants and a dress shirt that I had picked up at Goodwill and we were on our way to the Washington County Courthouse. When we entered the courtroom it was practically empty. There were a couple of attorney's towards the back but for the most part we would be arguing our case without an audience. Like at Qadira's trial what was missing were regular people who understood the law who were monitoring the process. It's easy for the judges and lawyers to break the law when the citizens have no clue as to what is really going on in the courtroom. We are trained to depend on lawyers to guide us and protect us but we forget that the legal system is also a business. People need their jobs and have to make money to survive so there can be no justice rendered. And Judge Donald R. Letourneau was about to make my point.

He came into the room with an attitude. He was angry at Renee before he ever even sat down. Nike is Oregon's golden calf and Letourneau wasn't about to be on the hook for biting the hand that feeds him. But the subject matter obviously bothered him and Nike's response didn't make things any better. To say that what had occurred was just a "bunch of crude jokes" and for the Nike attorney's to make him look like an ass in his own courtroom was making steam trickle out of his ears. When Renee got up to speak managing to refute in a very reasonable, polite manner each and every one of Nike's arguments Letourneau looked livid.

More and more people were starting to pile into the courtroom and this case was making him look ridiculous. What were two lawyers from the largest law firm on the West Coast doing in his courtroom with Nike and some young looking man talking about grown men dry-humping each other on the Nike campus? He was visibly disgusted with the whole thing but he was determined to do as he was told, and he had his marching orders. He was determined to follow the money. All he had to do was ignore everything Renee said and grant summary judgment. Maybe he felt a twinge of guilt for a brief second because as he granted the motion without any real explanation as to why he was doing it he did say he felt sorry for what had happened to Renee. The entire hearing had only lasted, maybe, 20 minutes; all that paperwork and work. Was it over? SLAP, KICK, PUNCH!

As the gavel hit the desk Renee just sat there stunned. We had never made a plan B. Design was his life and it felt like the door had been slammed tightly shut, locked, and the key thrown into the abyss. I told myself to get up and go to him. Letourneau was taking a tone with Renee. He was telling him to get out of his courtroom but Renee was just sitting in his chair looking like a deer caught in headlights. "Renee" I said loudly as I put my hand on his shoulder "We have to go." I wasn't sure where we had to go but I knew we needed to get out of there. I quickly started to gather our things.

Erin Potempa, Runkles, and Pederson had disappeared without a trace in the few little moments that it had taken me to reach my husband's side. The few people that were still in the courtroom looked confused. Judge Letourneau had quickly exited the room after telling Renee to get out and the two of us must have been quite a sight for those that had witnessed the hearing. I hurt all over but my poor husband was obviously devastated. What to do in the face of such blatant disregard for the law? We would have to figure out how to appeal the decision but first we had to wait for Letourneau's opinion and order.

DARK CLOUDS

So it was back to Qadira. We kept being told over and over that we needed a police investigation to get anything done but despite contacting just about every official we could think of nobody would lift a finger to help us. I had recently discovered the Independent Police Review and on March 11th 2009 we filed a comprehensive complaint with them explaining what had happened to Qadira, the trial, and the fact that the Portland Police were refusing to investigate.

SLAP, KICK, PUNCH! They hastily disregarded our complaint and then barred us from taking our complaint to the Citizens Review Board because there had been no "formal investigation." They were as cold as ice. The money had soldiers everywhere. What were all these so-called agencies for? What were all these people getting paid to do? Nobody even attempted to do their jobs. Who were they protecting? And what was the point in treating us so badly?

It was literally blow after blow after blow after blow. It was so difficult to grasp the fact that the entire system we had been raised in simply did not exist. Everything seemed so meaningless in this new world we had arrived in. There didn't seem to be anything here for us or our children. But were we just supposed to go and die? What was the point of the society we were living in if the laws didn't mean anything to the people you were supposed to be enforcing them?

Washing my own dishes had become one of the most difficult tasks because I had to do so facing Aimee McQuiston's mother's house which just happened to be the first house on the right on the street directly in front of my kitchen window. Can you believe that? There were days when I could just hear by blood boiling in my veins. It was so maddening! Keeping up the facade that everything was just great was not working out so well. But what else could we do? Nobody wanted to hear about our problems. Period point blank Nobody cared about us.

The kids complained that all we ever talked about was the "cases." This thing had virtually taken over our lives. We were constantly getting into loud conversations trying to go over every detail. We steadfastly looked at every fact. Was there something we had missed? Something we hadn't done? An "I" or a "T" we hadn't dotted or crossed?

And on May 26th 2009 we weren't even surprised to receive notice that Letourneau had dismissed the case with prejudice without opinion or explanation. We were starting to get the picture but even then we still held out hope that somehow things would work out. We told ourselves over and over that we just needed to put the case in front of more people. Somebody had to care. There had to be a way out of this place. There was no way we were going to survive in this strange new world. We filed a notice of appeal. We kept on knocking on doors. We kept calling lawyers. We kept researching the law. And we kept pissing people off.

It was around this time that in the midst of my despair that I found a small rock sitting on my bedside table with an inscription that that said "now faith is the substance of things hoped for, the evidence of things not seen." We couldn't figure out where that little rock came from but I knew it was a bible quote. Somehow it made me feel better just to sit on my bed staring down at it. Due to its mysterious appearance in our lives I tried to keep it close. I often found myself holding it in my hands just wondering where God was.

A few days later there was another slap in the face just for good measure. They were determined to beat the shit out of us. SLAP, KICK, PUNCH! Now Internal Affairs was jumping on the bandwagon also abusing their authority by declining to investigate Qadira's burn injury or the circumstances surrounding the trial. Why? Why were they doing this to us? These people were obviously trying to drive us crazy. Why not just investigate and make a determination about what happened. What the hell? Why all the runaround. Qadira was a child! Lord have mercy.

How could all of these seemingly professional institutions that we trusted to be administering the law turn their back on a burned up child? It was positively mind boggling the reach Rex Burkholder seemed to have. How was any of this even possible? We couldn't even find one appellate attorney to even consider taking Qadira's case and the clock was ticking. We made so many phone calls and knocked on so many doors our knuckles and eardrums were practically bleeding.

It was such a relief when on July 24 2009 Renee was able to retain Andy Simrin to represent Qadira. Maybe this rock was a good luck charm after all! Did we dare to hope again? He was your typical Birkenstock wearing, old building dwelling, dog loving Portland hippie that was to be our savior. He told us that appeals were very technical and he basically disregarded the things that Scott and Richard had hidden. He said that what they had done was really of no consequence on appeal. He had to concentrate on very specific errors that had occurred at the trial. This was a whole new process he said. Okay it wasn't that the system was broken, we just needed the right kind of help to make the system act right. So we decided to try again. The appeal had to be filed by September so we had very little time.

It was going to cost 10,000 dollars and we were broke but just the idea of ending this ordeal propelled us to turn over every stone in search of the money that would make Andy help us. Borrowing the money was a long shot but we couldn't bear to just give up on our daughter. We had already had to borrow 10,000 dollars from my sister when we finally decided to give up on trying to sell the house. We had come very close to losing the roof over our head and had to play catch up with the bank. The legal fees associated with fighting Nike had put us in a really bad position when the house did not sell, and we had been headed straight into foreclosure. But giving up meant Qadira's case was over and that wasn't an option we could seriously entertain.

My brother Soni reluctantly loaned us the money. He was wary of our pursuits but he was also convinced that there was a system and within that system there was justice. The whole family felt terrible about what happened and there was a definite consensus that something wrong had happened. They still really didn't understand what had happened but if there was chance it could be righted somehow then my brother was willing to help. It didn't really seem like too much of a long shot. How could an adult injure a child and just walk away without taking any responsibility at all? It was like we were living back in slaveholding America.

How could Qadira have to have gone through something like that and have nothing to show for it? Even in our world of dysfunction it was difficult to stomach what had happened. Of course the appellate court would remand the case. Of course McShane and the jury got this one wrong. After all that had happened we still were still having trouble accepting that there was no system. McShane and Letourneau were just a couple of bad apples spoiling the bunch we told ourselves. And all of the other elected officials that had turned a blind eye? Well they had little influence on the legal system. We made excuses to keep some semblance of the world we knew alive.

And so the time dragged on and on. It's all just one big blur really. We held onto the hope that things would get better. We found ways to navigate through the system. We made friends at work. We cooked dinner and hung out with the kids. We would get into heated conversations about what had happened. I spent a lot of time reading all of the depositions over and over and pouring over all the paperwork that was piling up in our house.

Every time I looked at the information I learned something new. It was all so mind blowing it was difficult for my brain to process. I looked for anything to help me understand how we had ended up in this place. It was as if we had fallen into a dark pit with walls of glass. No way out, nowhere to go, but all the way down to the bottom until we disappeared. The more I learned about the things that had gone on behind our back in terms of our relationship with Scott the more depressed and angry I became.

Sometimes the only way out of my head was to drink until I passed out. I always felt so bad when the fog lifted. I didn't want my kids to see me this way but somehow we were shielding them from the ugliest parts of this thing. We accomplished this through honesty. They knew the whole truth which gave our actions meaning. We weren't just the way we were for no reason. They knew what we were being put through because they were being put through it to. I opened myself up to absorbing all the hateful energy that seemed to be directed at our family. SLAP, KICK, PUNCH! The evil beast kept coming. We couldn't allow this thing to destroy us. Instead of ripping our family apart we were all becoming closer. Everyone was pitching in to help each other along and by the grace of God we were, even under extreme emotional distress, managing to get by.

Once Qadira's appeal was filed all we had to do was more waiting and hoping. There was always plenty of time to plan my demise and those of the people around me if the world that I lived in couldn't be turned right side up again. It wasn't so hard for me to see why people resorted to violence in the face of injustice but that was not our path. We could have chosen that path at any time but instead we waited and waited and waited. This is how the system breaks you. If you do manage to assert yourself and make an attempt to access your rights then the law has another lethal weapon to throw at the average person, and that is time. Time enough for poverty, grief, and depression to destroy you before any decision is ever made, if a decision is ever made.

We made it through another Halloween, Thanksgiving, Christmas and New Year's. The holidays had become totally meaningless but we went through the motions because that was all we had ever been accustomed to. We tried to maintain some type of normal.

And In the meantime I was learning a lot. For one thing I learned that not all companies confronted with a sexual harassment claim behaved like Nike. While I was working as a security officer at Unified Grocers I got to witness how these situations typically go down between two low waged workers. See, one of the guys I was working with found himself on the receiving end of sexual passes initiated by another older male guard in our group. When he complained Unified's Loss Prevention swung fast into action. Meetings were canceled, shifts were changed. We were all questioned about what we knew. HR had a big meeting and the accused was fired the very next day. Of course we are just talking about two 10 dollar an hour workers. But it gave me some hope that maybe all was not lost on Renee's appeal.

Every day that a new day presented itself we tried to be optimistic that things would eventually change for the better. We held onto the hope that somehow the system wasn't completely corrupt. Whenever we could muster up the energy we contacted whoever and whomever but it was always the same response. But we kept trying because we needed the system to exist. It was all we had. We had been conditioned to believe in America and despite what had happened we were still holding out for its survival. Lots of stiff drinks, deep breathes, and small reminders. I was grateful that

Qadira had found a group of friends and that all the kids seemed to be doing so well despite all the stress in the house. Maybe God was with us after all?

Renee never had trouble believing. I don't know how he managed to keep believing. Somehow he never blamed God for anything. It was so flat out irritating! Every time I would complain that God had somehow done this to us Renee was always reminding me that none of this was God's fault. He said it was the people who chose to do this. He would gently remind me that God gave man free will and this is what these people had chosen to do with theirs.

Sometimes I would feel so mad when he would tell me this! After all, look at what was happening to us? Where was this God anyway? But he was right. We still had what was most important. Kamaya hadn't died, and Kymani and Qayden were chugging along. Qadira seemed to be okay. For those reasons I could see he had a point.

We put on the best show we could considering the circumstances. Looking back our saving grace was always the kids. No matter how out of whack the world seemed there was always something right with them. A reason to keep existing; something real to hold onto. A smile, a joke, a piece of art, even an argument that ended in laughter. We were still together and despite our situation we found time to give our kids some kind of childhood.

They got to use to us talking about the "cases." Loudly, quietly and all of the time we tried to make sense of what had happened to our life. We wished we could do more for them but our financial situation coupled with all of the legal work and our mundane security jobs seemed to offer more than snatches of time.

We would reminisce about Renee's time at Nike, sarcastically referring to when "he lived in the castle." Life was certainly different when we had the illusion of security. The longer this situation dragged out the harder it got to imagine any kind of future besides just getting by. Too bad we couldn't sell the house and downsize. Our 1,800 dollar a month mortgage felt like a boot on our neck. We could barely afford to pay. And to top it all off we absolutely hated where we were.

Everywhere we looked there were reminders of our old life. Todd and Aimee still lived right around the corner and I still ran into them sometimes picking the kids up at school. The swoosh was in our faces wherever we went. The whole town kind of smelled like a big pile of shit. Our home had turned into a lovely prison. We would have given anything to get away from it all.

It took time to figure out how to file the appeal against Nike but we did what we had to do. The work piled up around us and we always felt in order to move forward it had to be done. At the very least Renee deserved some type of opinion and order making sense of what had occurred. What laws had been applied? We were supposed to be living in America. Letourneau could have at least attempted to pretend to do his job. He could have tried to explain himself in some kind of way. But the truth was he had no explanation so he didn't even bother to try.

Judges are supposed to apply the law, not decide cases based on who has more money and influence. But we were naive to believe that anybody really cared about justice. We were just telling ourselves that we just had to get more eyes looking at this thing. We had tried filing a complaint with the Judicial Board of Fitness but that turned out to be a joke.

They simply dismissed the complaint against Letourneau as quickly as they had dismissed the complaint against McShane. It was a "good ole boys club" and the general public wasn't invited. But this was the system that we lived under and it was our only line of defense. We had to make the system work. We put all of our energy into the appeals process. After all there would be three judges instead of just one looking at what had happened to Renee and Qadira. We held onto the idea that common sense and reason would prevail. We were desperate to close this chapter in our lives.

As the month of May 2010 drew to a close I got notice from the Appellate court that Qadira's case had been referred to mediation. It had been nearly a year since Andy filed the appellate brief. This was good news to me as it signaled that maybe Lachenmeier was backing off. Maybe we would finally be able to get some closure. But my feelings of relief weren't allowed to last long. The mediator called my cell phone with an attitude on a bright sunny day while I was just pulling into work at my crappy security job. Already angry before I said hello she questioned me as to why we ever hired an attorney after Qadira was burned. The tone in her voice told me she felt we had no right.

My heart started thudding away in my chest. She said that Todd and Aimee were upset that we had put Qadira into counseling because they felt we had only done that to hurt their feelings. I was so confused! What the fuck? I was shaking all over. I scrambled to find the right words to respond. Was this woman kidding? How could she be so heartless? I thought this was supposed to be mediation but the woman on the other end of the phone didn't sound like much of a mediator. I didn't really know what to say. We were the ones who had taken care of Qadira after she was burned. We changed her bandages and comforted her. It was Qadira who had suffered, Qadira who was scarred for the rest of her life.

Why this woman felt it was her job to take up for Todd and Aimee I did not know but this conversation was stirring up a sickness in the pit of my stomach. She basically told me to "go to hell" because Todd and Aimee were under her protection as well as the courts. It was like she had only called to try to make me feel bad for hiring Scott and pursuing anything on Qadira's behalf. Never mind Scott had lied to me the entire time.

I was shaking all over. At the end of the conversation she was yelling at me in obvious anger and I could barely get a word in edgewise. I could see that this so-called mediator had made up her mind well before she dialed my number. What were we supposed to do? Here I was being made to feel like I had to explain my actions as if I had done something wrong.

Everywhere we tried to find resolution doors were slammed in our faces by the very people who were supposed to be helping us. Nobody had any sympathy for what had happened to Qadira, and certainly nobody had any sympathy for us. By the time I got off the phone I felt like I was having heart palpitations and I had to find a way to calm down since I now had to walk into work and pretend that everything was fine.

It seemed like when it came to Qadira and Renee there was nothing but bad news. Sometimes jumping off a bridge just seemed like the best idea. I was so tired. I didn't have a very good feeling about the upcoming oral arguments in front of the appellate judges. This was all just a bunch of bullshit and I was up to my ears in it. Why would the so-called impartial mediator be acting like Todd and Aimee's personal bulldog? How could Rex Burkholder have this much influence? His reach seemed endless and suddenly I felt like a speck of dust floating around in a sea of fire.

The days came and went but I hardly noticed anymore. It was just one heartbreak after another. Life was just work, work, and work. At this point Haley was really the only friend I ever saw anymore. She would pop by bringing wine and snacks and I would listen to her tell me about the world I didn't live in anymore. We both shared a sense of guilt about the night when Renee had told us what had been happening at work.

We had both sat there and encouraged him to complain and Haley had seen what that had done to us. Not that either one of us could have ever imagined that our advice could have led to any of this but the world becomes a very lonely place when you don't fit in with the image of the status quo. Haley remembered how well things had been going for us before our world imploded.

She could still fit into a world that was getting harder and harder for me to recognize but she still wanted me to be able to participate so her and I could hang out. When Renee worked at Nike I had more access to society. I could meet her for sushi, go shopping, and get my hair and nails done occasionally. Looking back now I think she was waiting for that other Karellen to show up but that woman had packed her bags and checked out months ago.

It was a relief when July of 2010 finally came and with it Qadira's appellate hearing. I don't know why but there was still a part of me that dared to hope for some kind of end to this thing. To finally be relieved of the responsibility that Scott had piled onto my shoulders. At least some acknowledgement that what had happened was not okay. My wishes seemed reasonable to me. The stress of what happened to Qadira coupled with what had happened to Renee was just way too much. Please God.

I found myself just begging God for this all to be over. If we could get some kind of closure regarding Qadira's burn then it would be easier to hold onto the idea that there was a light at the end of the tunnel. Despite all that happened, it would signal that our life still had some order to it and that there was some kind of point to the society that we existed in. I didn't really care to live in a world where it was just okay to play naked games with little kids and burn them with tea kettles. I just wanted my authorities to act like they had some sense so I could start moving forward again in a world that I could make sense of. But when we arrived in Salem my feelings of dismay seemed to grow with each passing minute.

When we hired Andy Simrin over a year ago he had appeared to me as very nice down to earth guy who just wanted to help. But today for some reason he looked like a slimy snake oil salesman. His hand in mine felt sweaty when he greeted me with a nod and a handshake. He didn't look the way I remembered him. In his suit and tie I was taken aback at how much he reminded me of Scott. The harsh tone the mediator had taken with me just a few weeks ago was ringing in my ears.

We had seen fat Rudy driving beside us on the way down to Salem and now he was standing just a few feet away. My anxiety had manifested into an energy that I could see and touch. Like a thick smoke it was filling up my chest cavity making it hard for me to breath. And once again I could see the black robes filling in their allotted seats. Schuman, Wollheim, and Rosenblum reporting for duty.

They all looked very official but the minute they started talking I knew there was nothing official about any of them. They were there to do a job and they ruled in Aimee's favor faster than I could make sense of what was happening. SLAP, KICK, PUNCH! It was another shock to my system. Seriously what the fuck was going on!?

We were going to have to stop at the liquor store on the way home in order for me to swallow the lump that had risen in my throat. And they didn't even have the decency to say why. Now on top of the first 8,000 we owed the people who burned up our daughter, here they were again, granting Aimee an additional 610.00 dollars for all the trouble we had apparently caused her by choosing to appeal the initial unfair ruling. It was downright maddening! I imagined going to Todd and Aimee's house and gunning them down.

I was horrified at the utter, complete disrespect for the system that the judges displayed. They had no right to disregard the law when it was their job to apply it. How? Why? I had more questions than answers. And then out of nowhere came the "smoking gun."

I was already living in an alternate universe and it was hard to take my meaningless crappy job seriously and after showing up late several times I managed to get myself fired shortly after we lost Qadira's appeal. This, quite frankly was fine with me. My mom and sister wanted me back at the time anyway so it all worked out. Taking care of elderly dying people was very difficult but working for my family gave me more flexibility in my day. It was due to this turn of events that I just happened to be working back at Benchview Place when

Dr. Phil did a show on "guardian ad litems." Believe it or not it had never occurred to me to even Google the definition of the very job I had been appointed to do. The subject matter instantly caught my eye. I wasn't a fan of Dr. Phil but my sister liked to turn him on and so during the shift change that day his show happened to be playing in the background.

Typically I would have turned the channel immediately but today he had my full attention. What exactly was a guardian ad litem? No one had ever really explained it to me. So I was in for another big shock. Apparently they are licensed court appointed special advocates or licensed attorneys' who are only appointed to represent the best interests of the child in cases of abuse and neglect. They perform all types of duties in the criminal court that I did not perform in Qadira's case (because I had no clue what was going on) but generally they are the voice of the child with many judges adhering to their recommendations.

Now I knew that Scott had flat out lied to me but this was just so over the top! This meant even the judges had been lying to me as well as a whole bunch of other people. Andy had just stolen our money. Why would he do that? Oh my God what was wrong with everyone? The truth was staring me directly in the face. I simply was not qualified to have been Qadira's guardian ad litem. Period point blank. Scott had me fill the role so they could pull the wool over our eyes. I now had proof that the whole trial was fraudulent and our family had been taken for one big long ride. This was absolute insanity! How on earth could they pull this kind of crap in a court of law?

And believe it or not here we were getting the runaround from the police and the FBI after trying to file a report. These so called law enforcement officials would sit across from me as I told them the whole story and the only job they saw fit to perform was to play dumb. And the FBI agents never wanted to give us a name. Here I was a citizen of supposedly the greatest nation on the planet and I was forced to report my problems to an empty robot wearing a suit? It was hard to believe that things had really gotten that bad? No one on this planet seemed to have an ounce of integrity? Hi, where is the world I signed up to exist in? One agent declared "I'm not afraid of you!" Like what the hell did that mean? I was so fed up with the bullshit I had no problem getting loud with these people. I felt like I was yelling at my own kids? I faced my adversaries without fear because I was too tired to be afraid anymore.

And in August of 2010 after turning over every stone and boulder I could trying to get somebody to do something about all of this I followed in my husband's footsteps filing suit against Vangelisti Kocher claiming legal malpractice, professional negligence and emotional distress. This was a knock down dirty fight and I wasn't about to back down. I kept begging the FBI to investigate and one day they finally had a well-mannered agent tell me that he was going to turn all of our information over to the violent crimes unit. I wasn't going to be holding my breath waiting on them.

I petitioned the Court of appeals for the appointment of a lawyer for Qadira so we could petition the Oregon Supreme Court to review her case but they denied the petition. SLAP, KICK, PUNCH! I had absolutely resolved to leave no stone unturned in order to elevate Qadira's case to the highest levels. She was a child. Surely someone would show her some mercy. In my mind I was doing my patriotic duty. I should have been used to disappointment at this point but every time we got a new bogus ruling it hurt like hell. Nobody cared. So I was on my own again.

I just couldn't understand how a child could be treated so horribly by so many unforgiving adults? I went ahead and wrote up the petition using my position as Qadira's guardian ad litem. It may not have been legal but technically it gave me the ability act on her behalf within the legal system and I couldn't live with myself if I didn't at least try. The courts tactic was to drive me mad by openly refusing to acknowledge any of the issues that I raised. The days were longer and more stressful. My hair was falling out in clumps and more and more I needed some kind of alcohol to feel like I wasn't going totally crazy.

We were looking forward to the bleakest of holidays and once again on December 23rd 2010 we got slapped down hard again when we received notice that Chief Judge Paul J. De Muniz of the Oregon Supreme Court had declined without explanation or opinion Qadira's petition for review. Just one word: "Denied." And then to pour even more salt in the wound just a few days later on December 29th we received another ruling from the appellate court from Judge Haselton, Judge Armstrong, and Judge Duncan affirming Letourneau's ruling. Once again we had no opinion. No reason why we had been denied our right to a trial, no reason or explanation of any kind. Just one word: "Affirmed." SLAP, KICK, PUNCH! With little to no chance of success now Renee would have to follow in my footsteps and petition the Oregon Supreme Court to review his case. That too was to be soon denied. No opinion, no explanation. Such was their power to deny us any kind of resolution. It was a brutal psychological assault.

So we fought back with Justice for Qadira. We put up a website in order to get people to understand what we were going through. We made a huge sign, 9 feet by 5 feet and hung it on our front porch. It had a huge picture of Qadira's burned up leg and it said "Ask the State of Oregon why it's covering up child abuse?" And it had our website address: www.justiceforqadira.org, for the entire world to see. We published all the depositions and the trial transcript on our website and made flyers that looked just like the sign and handed them out all over town. We petitioned governor Kitzhaber on change.org and set up a Facebook page to garner some support. We couldn't just let them get away with what they were doing. The judges involved in covering up this thing should have to step down along with all of the elected officials who were unwilling to own up to what happened here. They had no business continuing to make decisions in our society. Where was the integrity and accountability? America is supposed to be a nation founded on laws.

But we were naive once again to believe that anyone would care or even be slightly alarmed by what we had discovered. We got slapped down hard all over again and again. SLAP, KICK, PUNCH! Everyone ignored us. Nobody even knocked on our door to check and see if we were okay. People smiled in our faces but I think secretly they just wanted us to go away and die. The authorities ignored us, the media looked the other way, our neighbors saw the sign and just drove on by, and only a small handful of people even bothered to sign our petition. Why in the world didn't anybody care about what happened to Qadira?

It was hard to get people to understand what we were going through in a society where no one had any idea of the legal process. It was actually easier for people to continue to believe that Todd and Aimee won the case and we were crazy. And for those who knew about our case against Nike they just thought we hadn't done something right and lost because we had represented ourselves.

Somehow what had happened to us must be our entire fault. People simply couldn't wrap their minds around the fact that the system could be that broken. It was a terrifying prospect that people did not want to accept. Even we kept hoping that it wasn't the truth. It was crystal clear how easy it was for judges and lawyers to behave however they wanted before an uninformed public. And more was set to come.

On March 14 2011 it was another devastating BLOW when we received a letter from Agent Glenn G Norling (whomever he was) telling us to never contact the FBI ever again. Go away they were telling us. Go away and die. SLAP, KICK, PUNCH! What more could they do to us now? At this point they had already taken everything away? We called all the way up to Washington DC to report to the Inspector General. Certainly somebody in DC would have to care. But wouldn't you know the people up there were hanging up on us. SLAP, KICK, PUNCH!

All my husband had to do was say his name and click. We sent the Inspector General a written report and were once again told that no one would even bother to investigate. Here we were living in modern day America with everyone around us celebrating the world's first black president and I was filled with a growing distrust of every single person in a position of authority. We had already been thoroughly disillusioned when Obama first ran president in 2008. After the trial it all seemed pointless. My mother had begged us to vote for him and we had but we hadn't found any change we could believe in.

In fact things couldn't be any worse. It now seemed every official we encountered was wearing an invisible pair of horns. Something very evil seemed to have taken over every institution in America and there didn't seem to be any way to stop it. The idea that Obama was the Antichrist wasn't so farfetched. He certainly hadn't done a damn thing for us when we wrote him.

Everything was beginning to stink of sulfur. All I could see was just an empty suit who spent most of his time lecturing everybody about stuff he knew nothing about. He really began to irritate me. Another elected mouthpiece for the establishment. Here we were being slapped in the face over and over and over again by our very own government and I had to listen to him run his mouth in the background like he was some type of God.

Every time we made a move they kicked us and beat us to the ground. We didn't have anything to look forward to because our whole world had been turned inside out. It was painfully obvious that they had already decided that nobody was going down for this. We simply weren't worth it. How many fake, fraudulent bullshit trials were they pushing through the courts on a yearly basis? Sounded like big business to me.

I read a story about a woman here in Oregon named Dawna Bigelow. She had been sentenced to 7 years in prison for burning a child she was babysitting. She claimed to have "accidentally" dipped the baby's face in some scalding water. She wasn't related to a politician so didn't get to "opt" for the civil trial that Aimee had been offered. She got her children taken away, 70 months in prison, and had to pay over 7,000 dollars of restitution. The case had been tried in the criminal court just a couple of months after the fraudulent trial that we had been subjected to. I thought about contacting her but what would I say?

I didn't agree with what she had done but as long as the law was extending forgiveness to some then I felt it should (at the very least) be extended to all. As my husband so eloquently stated in one of the briefs we filed with the court "equal application of the law is the cornerstone of a free and just society." It really burned us up inside to witness the blatant misuse and abuse of the law. People's lives were being turned upside down and inside out by a judiciary that only applied the law when it was convenient? Covering up the abuse of Qadira was just fine? We were just supposed to suck it and up and forget all about what they did to us? No acknowledgement, no apology, no compensation, no nothing?

Scott and Richard had with impunity lied straight to our faces and thrown our daughter under the bus. Why? They had no right. We kept looking for an attorney to help us but the legal community obviously had its marching orders. Greg Kafoury the famous civil rights attorney who claimed to have worked for Martin Luther King's Southern Christian Leadership Conference threatened me telling me "it's not going to end well for you or your family" right before he slammed the phone down hard in my ear. SLAP, KICK, PUNCH!

Under no circumstances were we to be helped. The last attorney I met with before ending my search told me all of my claims were just "fluff" and then tried to convince me to give her Power of Attorney over me like I was incapacitated and had no idea what I was doing. What the fuck? It was a unified front. I was fed up talking to one ass-clown after another and I was faced with litigating the lawsuit on my own.

I had learned enough from helping Renee file his suit against Nike and somebody had to hold Vangelisti Kocher accountable for what they had done. Why would they have lied to me like that? And why would the court just go along with it? I simply had to have my questions answered. There was no way we could go on without knowing the truth. These people had tried to destroy our family and I wanted to know why. Vangelisti Kocher hired James Callahan of Callahan and Shears to defend against me. Scott and Richard certainly had no trouble finding representation. It was going to be a brutal battle. I had to buckle down and go back over everything that had happened in the first case.

Going back over it all again made me want to curl up into a ball and die. SLAP, KICK, PUNCH! It was so horrible what they had done. By now Renee and I had picked out a cliff near my favorite spot on Mount Hood to drive off of if the time came when we both decided we couldn't take anymore. At this point we were so bloodied and bruised there were plenty of days when we just felt like giving up. We actually imagined packing up the kids and just making a final break for it. I didn't care for the kind of world we were living in anymore and I certainly didn't want my children to have to experience life here. This was just a bunch of bullshit.

We were no longer sure why we got up in the morning, or sent the kids to school, or did anything for that matter. We didn't even know where we were anymore. Every time we got to the top of one mountain another one would appear. All we could do was continue to confront these matters head on so we could really understand what was happening in the world we now had a permanent residence in. If my family was going to have to live here I had to keep digging until I could see the whole picture. That was one of the reasons we couldn't give up the fight when everyone around us was telling us it was over. Everyone we knew told us to give up but we just didn't know how. Giving up was a death sentence. This was madness!

I wanted someone to explain to me why any of this shit was okay. What Todd and Aimee had done, what Randy had done, what Nike had done, what all of our elected officials had done. Why were things being handled the way they were being handled? I had burning questions that needed answers. I knew the system was broken but at the very least I thought we had a system. But now we were coming face to face with the fact that there was no system at all. My government was literally being ran by a bunch of out of touch, over-privileged, spoiled brats who thought it was amusing to mess with people's lives.

There was no system yet we were all supposed to be depending on the system? How that was even supposed to work? Surely someone somewhere had to do something about this. But everyone seemed too frightened to do anything about any of it. Nobody even wanted to talk about it. We went to our elected officials and tried to alert the media to all the corruption we had found but it was a unified front. A loud deep silence had settled over the city of roses.

And Renee was still applying for jobs at Nike just because he could. After all he had just been laid off according to them. He should have been able to get a job but instead the state preferred for the taxpayers to cover our bills. We had been cast down with the untouchables and unable to make ends meet with both of our jobs we were stuck on food stamps and the Oregon Health Plan. And it wasn't like Renee was in danger of resuming his career any time soon. Nobody would help us.

He had just been exercising his rights when he sued the company and he should have been able to still be considered for a job according to the law but Nike was having none of it. Applying for more jobs also meant he could file more EEOC charges every time they refused to consider him for a position. We were desperate to get even a small piece of our old life back. Not to mention Renee was just wasting all of his talents stuck doing security when he should be designing. It wasn't fair at all.

He filed three more charges of retaliation and race discrimination with the Equal Employment Opportunity Commission. By now we were 100% sure that the agency was just another fake agency put in place so certain types of people could have a place where they could pretend that they worked. Wealthy people and their children who couldn't be bothered to break a nail, the kind of people who get up every day to collect a paycheck pretending to do a job that doesn't really exist so they can avoid doing any real work on the planet. It was utterly apparent that EEOC investigators make a ton of money to protect the corporations not the average individual trying to make enough to make ends meet. We were well aware the chances that the EEOC would act in our favor were very small but we couldn't help but entertain the benefit of the doubt.

Maybe somebody somewhere would show us some kind of mercy. Besides once they dismissed the charges we would be able to sue again. This time we vowed not to make the mistake of going to the state courts. What else could we do? We were constantly on the verge of losing everything. We had virtually no money to speak of and everyday was a tightrope balancing act. Each new situation was an opportunity for the other side to act right and play fair, out of respect for the process we so pretend to cherish in this country. The very process we all use as one of the main reasons we send our sons and daughters to die in the name of freedom. My brother was doing a tour in Iraq and I felt this feeling acutely. How dare these people disregard the law with impunity and how dare everyone around me not care.

I couldn't wait to do depositions in the case I had filed against Scott. Just the thought of getting that sniveling piece of no good filth to sit before me and answer my questions was enough to get me through to see another year. I wanted to look him dead in the eye so he could see he didn't break me. I wasn't the stupid, naive, uneducated little girl he thought he had taken for a ride in 2008. He had not gotten the best of me or my daughter. Our family and friends thought we had both gone totally crazy. But I was mad at most of them anyway for failing to understand what I was up against. Nobody ever seemed to get it. I got super tired of trying to explain the situation and they all got tired of hearing about it. At first my friends began to keep their distance and now I kept mine because I was having trouble understanding the utter and complete complacency that surrounded me.

Even my own family who was watching us go through it couldn't seem to understand. It was infuriating! It was easier for people to think we had done something wrong than for them to conceive of the idea that the system had imploded right before our very eyes. Operating in a superficial environment became very difficult. I had difficulty sitting through mindless conversations that made my head want to explode. The news began to irritate me. Everything looked so meaningless and fake. All these reporters, talk show hosts, and elected officials that I had tried to contact and none of them wanted to cover what had happened here. If they could keep us covered up then what else were they hiding? The world didn't make sense without a system and being faced with dismantling and rebuilding a whole new one was a daunting a task for people to grasp. So we got tuned out.

I used all of my available time to put the case against Vangelisti Kocher together. I gathered all the available info and read it over and over until my eyes bled. I spread everything out in front of me and became a detective. I became convinced that something had gone terribly wrong at the hospital on the night of April 12th 2007 and I went back to the Providence St. Vincent emergency room and started asking questions. I requested copies of Qadira's records from the night of the burn and people in the records department at Providence looked a little shaken and scared. I couldn't figure out what all the worried looks and tight lipped responses were all about but I was determined to get to the bottom of it. I was told emphatically by one of the male nurses that in cases of suspicious injury to a child "We investigate!" Yeah right you investigate I thought to myself. These people and their "Filthy" bed of lies. How could they sleep at night?

I requested a copy of the Department Of Human Resources report that had been generated when we had been visited by the social worker after the trial. This report was fishy as well. Parts of it were whited out. The worker had never visited with Todd or Aimee nor did she ever even set foot in their house. Fat Rudy had apparently told her that we were on welfare and angry and some other whited out stuff and for that she closed the case as "unable to determine" for child abuse on November 6th 2008. Like what exactly could she not determine?

Ironically just days after discovering this little fact I was denied a copy of Qadira's police report because it "contained reports of child abuse." I was having one "What the fuck" moment every time I turned around.

We never had a chance at winning the trial because the whole thing had been a fraud. Why? Why? Why? Why did they do this to us? Fake, Fake, Fake! The jury was a fraud and I suspected that Susan Glosser was nothing more than a plant to help the whole charade run smoothly. What else would a professor from Lewis and Clark be doing as the head juror in such a case? It was all starting to make a very bizarre sort of sense.

Scott, Richard, Rudy, Judge McShane, they had all been working to cover up a crime. Now I know I have said this before but now I was 100% sure and my mind was blown! It was clear that everyone that we had encountered after the trial was just doing their job to protect the system but I couldn't figure out why. And there were just so many of them. Why? Was it for money? Why were they working so hard to protect something that was so totally useless?

All I could do was hope that the next judge I stood before had a conscious or at the very least a sense of duty to our country. I often thought back to the dream I had with Qadira and the snake. I looked up the King Cobra and was surprised to learn that it was associated with Lord Shiva, the destroyer. The picture was slowly coming together. I knew for sure that if anything needed to be destroyed if was this terrible system.

I thought about pushing that old green couch aside and how I felt when I found myself staring down at all the petrified shit trying to comprehend how it got there and how to clean it up. Maybe my dream wasn't a dream. Maybe it was a vision of things to come because there seemed to be shit all over the place. I looked up Judge David F. Rees on the internet. His profile said he was from San Francisco. He looked young and liberal. I held out hope that he would have the courage to turn this thing around.

On April 7th 2011 Vangelisti Kocher filed their motion for Summary Judgment and I knew what time it was. They just wanted this whole thing to go away despite the fact that all of the facts were in question. Their strategy was just like Nike's. Deny, deny, deny. Leave all of the material facts in question and expect the judge to do exactly as he was told. I filed a comprehensive opposition to their motion and waited for the showdown. I was ready to give this judge a piece of my mind.

I showed up to the Multnomah County Courthouse ready for anything. Sure I was wearing the same old hand me down Goodwill clothes that I had in my closet for years but I made the best of it. I knew for sure I wasn't nearly as grimy as the people who would be joining me in the courtroom that day. But on May 25th 2011 a positive turn of events left me feeling like there was hope for our legal system. Judge Rees actually appeared horrified at Callahan's assertion that the "guardian ad litem" didn't matter. He was having none of Callahan's argument in that regard and for a brief moment I could breathe a little easier. Could the law really be working? I walked out of that courtroom finally feeling vindicated. I knew that this country was corrupt but I also knew that there were Americans who were willing to stand up for what was right, I was proud of Judge Rees.

I now had another opportunity to amend my complaint and a judge that actually cared or so I thought. I tried to really focus. I wrote down everything that had gone wrong in Qadira's trial. For once and for all it looked like I was going to have the opportunity to get all of my questions answered. I could look Scott, Richard and whoever else I needed to in the eye and resolve this shit once and for all. But once again things were falling apart because suddenly Qadira wasn't looking so good. I felt like I was in an old Charlie Brown cartoon and there was a dark rain cloud that followed me and my family around. Many times I found myself cursing that old house that had entrapped us. Now, a new concern to grapple with?

Qadira's friend's mom had cornered me after a slumber party declaring that "Qadira was thin and peeing all the time." She said she wasn't trying to pry but she was a nurse and something didn't seem right. I felt a little defensive because my kids got regular checkups and Qadira had never missed an appointment. She was fine. She was okay. I did notice that she seemed to stand with her shoulders hunched over more lately but I attributed that to her coming of age as a teenager. Yes she was thin but we had chalked that up to her magic metabolism. It was a running joke in the family. And when Qadira got sick and was sent home from Outdoor School late in May of 2011 I had taken her to the doctor seeking answers. And on that particular day when her friend's mom cornered me Qadira had literally just been seen at OHSU's family clinic by her regular doctor Nancy Gorden-Zwerling who declared once again that she just needed rest and fluids. I told this to her friend's mom who didn't seem convinced.

And as it turned out that was her last visit to OHSU because shortly thereafter while in the midst of doing research in my case against Vangelisti Kocher my brain was finally able to process that they had labeled Qadira's burn injury as "accidental" in her official medical records without having done any investigation. There was a whole blurb in her medical record with an explanation of what had

happened that night that didn't match a word of what Todd and
Aimee had said at the trial.

It also told me that they had waited a whole hour to call us after
Qadira was burned. What the fuck? Todd took her down to the
basement and they waited a whole hour to call us? What was I
reading? I could not believe my eyes. What the hell was going on?
Here I was trying to gather as much information as I could to
determine how to proceed when I got the chance to question Scott
and Richard and every time I opened a new document I was being
shocked to all hell. I was aghast! So this was what the jury had been
looking at? Why didn't Scott tell me? Who determined this and
how?

When I questioned OHSU about where they had gotten their
information about what had occurred the night of the injury they
wouldn't give me any answers. I asked them to remove the
unsubstantiated information but they adamantly refused. On close
examination I now realized that Providence had also amended their
initial report from April 12th 2007 to reflect the false OHSU
assertion that what had happened to Qadira was an "accident." I
called all over the place demanding an explanation but no one wanted
to explain to me how they had come to that conclusion.

OHSU claimed that I said it was an "accident" and Providence
claimed that Qadira said it was an "accident." But I hadn't been
present when Qadira was burned and certainly anything she had said
in the short visits she had had with the doctors on the night of and
the day after she was burned did not count towards any type of
official determination. They had barely even talked to her! That I
knew for sure. She certainly hadn't given them the information that I
was looking at. The information in the OHSU record didn't even
match what Todd and Aimee had claimed had happened in their
depositions or at trial. Omg what the fuck!

I was positively fuming! How dare these people!? Qadira's injury
could only be ruled "accidental" after an official police investigation
which we had been repeatedly denied. Now I had two supposedly
reputable hospitals lying to me! Why? Doctors, lawyers, judges, law
enforcement officials just spewing diarrhea all up in my face! Who
the fuck did these people think they were? They put hands on our
naked burned up daughter and now they didn't think they owed us
any kind of explanation?

It was becoming increasingly clear how the jury had returned a no negligence finding. This was all bullshit! I imagined that even if all of the jurors hadn't been in on the cover-up they would have been an easy group for someone like Susan Glosser to lead around by the nose. Why would anyone dispute the findings of two reputable hospitals? These records suggested that there had been an investigation into what had happened to Qadira by the proper law enforcement when the fact was no investigation had ever taken place. It was a lot to wrap our minds around.

And in the middle of all this we were still trying to keep track of our kids and our life. Going to work, school, and everything else in between. Renee was still working security and I was still at Benchview. Taking care of the elderly was taking a tremendous toll on me. I was very very tired. I was confronted with death all of the time and to add to the strain of my job several of my aunts and uncles had also died since 2007. Talk about the walking through the valley of the shadow of death.

Qadira was now 11 years old and still the night of April 12th 2007 remained mostly a mystery. The sign with her bloody leg still hung on the side of our house and we sent her to Harriet Tubman Middle School for her 6th grade year. It was on the other side of town and a very diverse all girls public school so it was our hope it would help boost her confidence. A change of scenery had been absolutely necessary. The transportation was brutal because it was a daily commute from the Westside to the Northside but the hard work was paying off. She seemed to be doing pretty well despite everything that had happened and due to a newfound talent for languages she was becoming fairly fluent in Japanese. This was also thanks to a once a week tutoring lesson and constant self-study which had greatly brightened her spirits. A deep bond between the children was keeping the evil at bay.

I couldn't wait to depose Scott Kocher. I was itching to give that sniveling, no good lying sack of shit a piece of my mind. I wasn't afraid of Callahan or anybody and on April 22 2011 I finally got my chance. I resolved that I was going to make him talk in front of Qadira. He had thrown my daughter under the bus and he had better be prepared to tell it to her face. When I saw Scott for the first time I could feel the anger boiling in my chest.

He looked pale and cowardly and I was on fire. I had my

questions prepared and this time he was going to have to answer to me. His responses were cowardly, as he tried to lie his way out of what he had done. It took every fiber of my being not to reach across the table and snap his neck. Without Renee steady at my side and Qadira as my witness for good measure I don't believe I could have contained myself.

The first round of depositions ended with Callahan and Scott walking out in angry childish defeat as I grilled Scott repeatedly about his treatment of Qadira and our family. He couldn't take the heat and Callahan freaked out screaming and yelling at me and we had to reschedule. I decided not to bring Qadira back the second time. There had been too much evil in the room the first time around and I couldn't subject her to that again. On May 2nd I continued to ask the burning questions I had held for so long. I finally got Scott to admit that he had served on a committee with Rex Burkholder and confirmed that he had worked for Stoel Rives prior to taking on Qadira's case. Was Scott initially working for Rex or Nike?

I was trying to complete the puzzle and he was doing his very best to sidestep all of our questions. Due to mandatory reporting laws it had first legally been Providence's job to call the police on the night of April 12 2007. OHSU also shared that responsibility since I had taken Qadira to see them the very next day. But since they both had failed to do their jobs Scott certainly should have done it for them and informed us that they hadn't done it.

He had been Qadira's lawyer tasked with protecting all of her rights. When I questioned him as to why he failed to call the police he actually said to me it was because "people don't like having the police called on them." Well duh! It didn't take a Harvard education to figure that out. He was sniveling and pathetic and despite Callahan's best attempts it was difficult to defend someone who had engaged in such sorry behavior.

On May 27th I filed additional claims against Vangelisti Kocher claiming intentional, reckless, and negligent infliction of emotional distress. We had gotten very used to putting together legal briefs. Not exactly our idea of a good time but "The work" had to be done. Scott and Richard had known better.

They knew Qadira's case was supposed to be tried in criminal court. They were well aware of the pain they had caused our family. They did it all on purpose. Why? But again my questions were set to linger because when we were called to appear in front of Judge Rees again he turned on us. I could only assume the money had gotten to him. Suddenly the guardian ad litem issue wasn't an issue anymore and he was trying to tell me to take basically everything out of my complaint. SLAP, KICK, PUNCH!

There I was again standing in front of another judge getting his palms greased by the establishment acting like burning up a kid with a teakettle wasn't abuse. And acting like Scott pretending to be her lawyer and appointing me her guardian ad litem wasn't totally egregious! Every courtroom we walked into in this country was fake. Monsters in black robes robbing us of the rights our ancestors fought and died for. Disrespecting our men and woman in uniform every time they turned a blind eye to the freedoms we were supposed to enjoy. Just washing their filthy hands in a river of blood and laughing. It was maddening to watch them abuse their authority left and right.

They did it with impunity strengthening our resolve to keep up the fight. And I made sure to let each and every one of them have it. I started to call them all out. I wasn't going to take this shit lying down. When Callahan deposed me he spent two hours yelling at me and I yelled back. He dared to grill me as to why we hadn't called the police. Excuse me? Why we hadn't called the police?

First of all we were the only ones who had ever called the police. Sure it had been months down the road but that was only because everyone had taken it upon themselves to lie to us about every little single thing that they could. We were the only ones who had bothered to do anything for Qadira. We took care of her, we changed her bandages! She would certainly have died had we not done something. How dare he talk to me like that? He hadn't let Renee sit in on the deposition and we hadn't challenged him on that but Renee said he could hear us all the way from his position in the hall.

The next time Judge Rees started issuing yet another bogus ruling I stood up and started to ask him if he liked to play naked games with little kids and burn them with tea kettles. He was obviously embarrassed and tried quickly to move the process along as there were people filing into his courtroom. He didn't really want to have to explain to somebody or anybody why he was making an ass of himself.

The Almighty Dollar had spoken to him and through him. He was determined to do his master's bidding and he quickly directed me again to amend my complaint by removing all of my allegations, banged down his gavel and left the room. The filthy stinking criminal!!! When we walked out of the courtroom I turned on Callahan. "You got enough money greasing the back of your palms?" I yelled.

He stood there red faced. I flung a few more choice words in his direction as the security guards stood by watching. I just wished they would come and try to arrest me. I turned and made my way out of the courthouse with my heart pounding in my ears. At this point I had completely lost my fear of the system and all of the people running it. The only feeling I had left was disgust.

And our life continued on like a Charlie Brown cartoon with a perpetual storm cloud following us around raining down on our heads. When things appeared to be going in the right direction they never really were. We were totally surprised when on May 30th 2011 the EEOC determined that Nike had violated my husband's civil rights.

You think we would have been celebrating but at this point we knew better. What was Nike up to now? Once again they were offering us the 40,000 dollars. What was it about that number anyway? It reminded us of the promise of 40 acres and a mule given to the slaves. The number was very symbolic and they were not budging. And again we were left all alone trying to sort it all out. No attorney's, no anybody, just us trying to figure out what to do without any help or advice.

But the fact of the matter was the 40,000 dollars wasn't going to solve any of our problems. At that point all I could do with that money was maybe pay my brother and sister back. We had long ago stopped paying any bill that we could not afford. The debt was suffocating and the bill collectors were relentless. We had grown very phone adverse and nobody at our house ever really picked up anymore. We were going to have to keep fighting for something better. And we were still grappling with the fact that Renee and Qadira had been denied their constitutional rights in the court? It was a lot to think about.

But it all didn't matter anyway because a few days later when we got back to the investigator to ask some questions about the process the EEOC rescinded their determination. Now suddenly out of the clear blue, 4 years after he was fired, Nike was claiming that Renee "took" something. Like what? What the fuck? Here we were all the way in 2011 and now all of a sudden he took something? Like shouldn't they have brought that up way back in 2007? SLAP, KICK, PUNCH! We were floating down a never ending river of bullshit. At first the EEOC investigator refused to say what that "something" was. How could he keep that from us?

Renee kept pressing him and eventually he decided to give us at least that little bit of info. Nike was claiming that it was his portfolio. Really? The same portfolio Mac had encouraged him to put together after he was fired. The same portfolio that nobody at Nike had asked to look at before they threw him out with the trash 4 years ago. The same portfolio that nobody in the industry would look at. The same portfolio they had asked for during the initial litigation in 2008 and the very same portfolio that they had looked at and then returned to him in its entirety way back in 2009 after paying Judge Letourneau to do their dirty work.

You have got to be kidding me! We had to call bullshit on that one. And when we brought these facts up to the EEOC the original investigator who had given us the favorable outcome suddenly up and disappeared like a "fart in the wind" and a new investigator was assigned to the case.

The new investigator disregarded all of the facts and issued another 3 indeterminate findings. It was so maddening! There was no system. No recourse. No way to recoup what we had. No way to move forward and no way to go back. And the worst part was being awake in this alternate universe. Knowing that the entire system was a fraud but unable to really do anything about it. But we had to keep trying and on June 17th 2011 Renee decided to file yet again another lawsuit against Nike for race discrimination and retaliation.

All of the people involved in this thing had been able to keep their jobs and most of them now had promotions and raises and they were all white. The people who had helped beat Renee down were having the red carpet rolled out for them. The harder we fought, the more they got. SLAP, KICK, PUNCH! We had to make something stick. There just had to be a way to right this wrong.

When the 4th of July came round we were invited to a party out in

Estacada. We really wanted to go because at this point we didn't get out much. The few friends we still had kept their distance. No one really wanted anything much to do with us. We were mired in controversy and we didn't get many invitations to anywhere.

This was supposed to be a time to just be out in the country and relax but Qadira wasn't feeling well again. We thought she might start feeling better when we got out into the fresh air but as the hours ticked by the complaints got louder and louder. She kept insisting that if she didn't get some soda she would "die." We thought she was being a bit overly dramatic. We got busy setting up the tent and visiting old friends but as the hours passed by Qadira started looking really bad.

She wanted to leave. We couldn't even stay for the show. That was a shame because we had never been invited to something like this before. She was begging us and we were beginning to question the sanity of sleeping in a tent with a sick kid? We packed up and headed home.

What a time for one of the kids to be sick. It's not like we got out very often anymore. We resigned ourselves to watching whatever fireworks we could see from our porch. There would be no big show down by the river this year. That was okay. We were used to disappointment. But Qadira was acting so strangely. She was starting to really frighten us. It was like her life energy was draining out of her body all of a sudden and alarmingly fast.

We tried to get her to eat, tried to take her walking around the neighborhood to perk her up. This didn't seem just like the flu. We worried that maybe she just needed to eat but she refused. She seemed really confused. We worried that maybe this was some type of eating disorder that we had missed. She literally looked thinner and thinner as the hours rolled by. What were we missing? She slept close to me that night and just like when she was a baby I would check to see if she was still breathing. As the hours ticked by she looked worse and worse.

I had to be at work early the next morning so I left before anyone woke up. By 9:00 am Qadira was calling. She told me she needed to go to the hospital but Renee had left to go to the store. There was urgency in her voice. I called Renee on the cell phone over and over but he didn't pick up. I felt helpless because I had no car, no way to leave work. After a few minutes Qadira was telling me that Renee had walked through the front door.

I could hear Qadira exclaiming that she needed to go to the hospital "right now" and Renee was saying they were going to leave as soon as he put the perishables away. "Hand the phone to your dad." I said. The authoritative tone in my voice garnered an immediate response. "Renee, stop what you are doing and take her to the hospital." He had to admit she looked terrible but he was still carrying on about the perishables when suddenly she started to vomit all over the floor. We were all yelling now. It was obvious that he was not thinking clearly due to shock. He had admitted she looked really bad but he couldn't wrap his mind around the fact that there might really be something wrong with her.

He just kept saying over and over that Qadira did look really really bad. And if she looked any worse than when I had left in the morning I feared for her life. "Where should I take her" He asked. I couldn't think. Providence and OHSU were out. My brain was scrambled up. "Emanuel." Yes that's right. They had treated Kamaya. "Take her to Emanuel." I said firmly. And then the phone went silent. I had to hurry up and wait for whatever news came next. In moments like these I had to give myself over to the universe. I recognized this was just another situation where I had no control.

It was hard to focus at work but I just had to keep going through the motions. The nervous energy I was feeling was best used to do something productive in the moment. Answering bells, taking people to the bathroom, preparing lunch. I couldn't let the worry immobilize me.

I kept moving until Renee called for the second time with the news. He sounded all broken up. And my world was turned upside down again. "Karellen, she has Type 1 diabetes." "BOOM!" There was that sound again. I had become very familiar with the sound of my life falling apart.

It was just one life changing event after another. We never had time to recover from one shock to the next. And after work I was on my way to the hospital after stopping by the house to find Kymani cleaning up with a frantic look on his face. As I gathered up a few things he mustered up the courage to ask, his voice breaking. "Is Qadira going to die?" I looked at my boy. He had been stronger than I could imagine; poor kid. I wasn't about to give him any more bad news.

He was doing the best he could to help out with his brother and sisters as waves of tragedy washed over our family. He was standing strong. I went to hug him, to reassure him that Qadira was not going to die. We couldn't take that. I asked him to keep an eye on his little brother and sister. I wasn't sure what was going to happen but I was sure that my daughter was going to live. I could see at least that. It wasn't her time.

When I arrived Qadira was still in the intensive care unit in the ER. She was lying peacefully in her bed. She looked ashen and weak but she still managed a smile. She was taking the news better than her dad. She knew something had been terribly wrong. One of her doctors came in to say hello. He took the time to introduce me to the team of people that had stepped in to help save Qadira's life. He was trying to keep everything as upbeat as possible informing me of all the measures they had taken.

Most of what he explained to me went over my weary head but the conversation kept me occupied. Instead of focusing on all the machines and Qadira's fragile state my mind went to work trying to figure out everything he was telling me. It was a much needed distraction. After her blood sugar was stabilized she was finally admitted to the Children's hospital.

But something strange had happened when Renee had first brought her to the ER. One of the first things one of the nurses asked him was if she had ever experienced a trauma. Renee replied "She was burned." To that which the nurse replied "Was she treated here at our Burn Center?" Renee was shocked. I was shocked. We had never heard of any Burn Center.

But there it was right outside the window of her room. The Oregon Burn Center. I sat there by the window staring down at the building wondering what went on inside. Renee was determined to go and talk to somebody over there but first we had to learn all about Type 1 Diabetes. Qadira's whole life was going to be different now. Her pancreas was no longer functioning and she would have to learn how to give herself insulin and closely monitor her blood sugar.

In Type 1 Diabetes the body's immune system destroys the cells that produce insulin. Without insulin cells cannot absorb sugar (glucose) which they need to produce energy. We asked how this could have happened but the doctors didn't seem to really know. Nobody wanted to talk about the fact that she had been burned and they were throwing so much information at us our heads were spinning.

It seemed like there were so many things to remember just to keep our daughter alive. Not to mention one of us had to keep running home to take care of the other kids. In a world of 7 billion people there never seemed to be anyone to call on for help. It was so incredibly stressful. Everyone in our lives was busy managing their own islands and we had to juggle everything by ourselves.

And it didn't help to have Qadira's doctor's blatantly disregarding her health history but that was the boat we were in. At any mention of the untreated burn their faces would go blank and then a change of subject. SLAP, KICK, PUNCH! Nobody was going to admit anything.

We tried to stay focused on the task at hand but it was difficult when the people around us were disregarding our concerns. The daily shots, carb counting and blood sugar monitoring were all some of the new things that we had to grasp before she was discharged. It was up to us to be there for our daughter and once again we found ourselves stepping up the plate. Qadira's health was on us and arguing with these people wasn't going to solve anything.

And when we finally got a moment we paid a visit to the Burn Center where we visited with Dr. Joseph Pulito who told us that based on the diagnosis of the ER report from Providence St. Vincent Hospital the night Qadira was burned and the report from OHSU Hospital the very next day that Qadira should have been transferred to the Oregon Burn Center for treatment. Dr. Pulito seemed a little frightened to talk to us and I was reminded of our encounter with Judge Mark Gardener. It was like the man behind the curtain in the Wizard of OZ. Every person of authority that we encountered didn't really seem to have any authority. We wanted Dr. Pulito to help us better understand what damage Qadira may have incurred due to her untreated burn injury. Was the burn the reason she now had Type 1 Diabetes?

After all they had done nothing to stabilize her the night she was burned or in the days after. We had been sent home all alone. No fluids, no antibiotics, they hadn't even bothered to take her blood pressure or show us how to bandage the wound and with what. And the next day OHSU had done the same. What the hell was going on here?

It was finally dawning on us that the hospitals hadn't done anything at all to treat Qadira. And it hadn't been for lack of insurance because Renee had still been working at Nike at the time. Yet here we stood in a state of the art facility built especially to deal with these types of injuries and we were supposed to believe that the burn had nothing to do with Qadira's condition now?

Dr. Pulito's hands were shaking as he quickly examined the scar the burn had left behind. He was acting like he was a in a big hurry and he stuttered as he attempted to sidestep most of our direct questions. It was quite obvious he had his marching orders and that he intended to carry them out. SLAP, KICK, PUNCH!

I began doing research on burn injuries and was increasingly alarmed at what I found. From what I was reading it was becoming progressively clear that the lack of action taken by both hospitals after Qadira was burned should have killed her. I was finally beginning to understand.

The skin is the body's largest organ and a burn injury is an assault on the entire body. Just the shock to her body from the intense pain she endured could have killed her. The continuous rush of glucose that had invaded her body as a response to the burn was what had eventually burned out her pancreas. And we were lucky for just that. All of her organs had been under assault. That was a no brainer. A second degree burn is the most painful type of injury a person can sustain and our daughter had been left by multiple doctors to manage the pain with just a little bit of Tylenol.

Burn victims usually need a morphine drip to endure the searing pain that burns deliver. They are given rounds of antibiotics, vitamin D therapy, and placed on high calorie special diets and they are kept in extremely sterile environments. The risk of infection is very high and can be lethal. If the wound is on a joint, then special precaution should be taken to keep the injury immobilized and elevated. The wound is debrided to remove all of the necrotized flesh. All things no one did! In fact nobody had even bothered to call and check on her.

She had been sent home to die. Oh my God! Oh my God! I was horrified at what I was reading! It was in fact a miracle that she had survived. Even our best efforts should not have been enough. Burns are such serious injuries regular hospitals are not equipped to deal with them which are why there are Burn Centers in the first place. I was finally beginning to see the whole picture and it wasn't pretty.

How could two reputable hospitals leave a child to suffer and possibly die a terrible painful death? The pain Qadira had gone through was akin to the worst torture. I contacted the American Burn Association and was reluctantly told again that based on their recommendations Qadira should have been transferred to the Oregon Burn Center. But still no one wanted to help us or our daughter.

I was on the rampage again. I filed complaints with the Oregon Medical Board against all the doctors involved in Qadira's medical care. These people had lied to me and almost gotten my daughter killed and I wanted answers. But once again I wasn't surprised to have all of my complaints dismissed without investigation or explanation. SLAP, KICK, PUNCH!

Nobody from Providence would talk to me and when I finally met with a representative from OHSU he just made promises that he didn't intend to keep. I was told that all of Qadira's doctors were going to be brought into the room where they would be made to explain their actions but that never happened. A few days after the meeting with OHSU I received a letter from the hospital stating that they were happy to have been there for us in our time of need and there would be no meeting. It was positively mind blowing! We had been slapped in the face so many times our cheeks were numb.

Our next hope was to finally get some of these issues resolved by finally getting a chance at a trial against Vangelisti Kocher in front of a real jury. But we weren't feeling very optimistic about that. I had threatened to file a complaint against Judge Rees for directing me to remove all of the allegations from my complaint before allowing me to present any evidence. After all he was complicit in covering up the abuse of my daughter.

The only allegation he was going to allow me to keep was the last one which stated that I had been forced to hire an appellate attorney to continue helping Qadira after Scott had thrown her under the bus. And what exactly would have been the point of going to trial over that? I wasn't an idiot! Of course we didn't have to hire an appellate attorney. I could have just walked away but who else was going to stand up for my daughter, especially since I had been appointed her guardian ad litem.

And Renee was still fighting the State over the loss of his job. In conjunction with the race discrimination suit that he had filed against Nike he now had decided to file a federal lawsuit against the State of Oregon and all of the judges who oversaw the proceedings in his first case against Nike. There had to be a way to hold these people accountable for what they had done. The paperwork we were now dealing with was staggering. He had been denied his right to a trial and after all that we had lost and were continuing to lose he kept looking for ways to elevate his concerns.

Maybe the federal court was different? Maybe the judges in the federal court would actually be interested in doing their jobs? It was still entirely possible that once the fed's really found out how the state was overstepping its bounds that they would be looking to hold people accountable. For some reason we still held out hope on the idea that there was some kind of system and through our diligent efforts it could be found again.

So on August 15th 2011 after a stop at the federal courthouse so Renee could file yet another case it was on to the Multnomah County Courthouse for a meeting with Presiding Judge Jean K. Maurer and Callahan for a so-called status update conference on my case against Vangelisti Kocher. I never noticed back then how many things were all happening on the same day but it wouldn't be long before I was looking back with shock and wonder.

It didn't take long to realize that we had only been called to the Courthouse to be slapped in the face. SLAP, KICK, PUNCH as hard as they could. It was like the only strategy that these people seemed to have. Judge Maurer sat on her side of the table acting stupid and Callahan sat on his side looking like an ass. At one point Judge Mauer started acting like she was trying to settle things but their offers of 1000, maybe 2000 dollars were just meant to rub salt in an already large wound.

Renee and I just sat there trying to be reasonable but you can't reason with people who know they are above the law, but you can make them feel guilty with just your presence. The fact that we just kept showing up was enough to get under people's skin. Judge Mauer tried to act like she wasn't really all that involved but it was easy to see who she was working for. As the negotiations failed she pretended to do me a favor by appointing a new judge to the case. Judge Adrienne Nelson, who just happened to be the only black judge on the court. I had a brief flicker of hope.

But a quick meeting with Judge Nelson let me know what time it was. She was obviously put in charge to put me in my place because she came in reeking of attitude trying to tell me again to take all of my allegations out of my complaint. I went to Tubman Middle School and Jefferson High School and survived. I stood my ground. Her attitude did not scare me. I wasn't stupid! I wasn't taking anything out of my complaint when I had rock solid proof that everything that I was alleging actually happened. On September 14th when we met again she insisted again that I amend the complaint and granted Callahan's motion to strike all of my allegations.

Like all you have to do in America is ask the judge to not let the other sides allege what you did and suddenly you win your case? I could go to trial but I couldn't talk about any of the emotional distress that Scott and Richard had put me through by illegally appointing me my own daughter's guardian ad litem; Scott's connection to Rex Burkholder or Stoel Rives; The fact that Scott and Richard did not report Qadira's injury to the police to get a proper investigation done; The fact that Scott had illegally given my medical records to the jury which stated that I had anxiety to make me look crazy, or the fact that Qadira's case was a matter of child abuse and should have been tried in criminal court. SLAP, KICK, PUNCH!

In fact I wouldn't be able to say anything about anything that Scott did or Judge Nelson could hold me in contempt and have me arrested. What was the point? The only reason I was left holding a card was because I was acting as my own attorney and she had no way to force me to comply. I had to amend my complaint. She couldn't do it for me. Callahan actually tried to offer to do it as if I didn't know what was going on. He took my complaint and drew a line with an arrow to the only allegation that they were going to let me keep. It was the one that stated that I had had to spend 10,000 dollars to hire Andy Simrin to protect Qadira's rights after Vangelisti Kocher threw her case. But I had a right to present my entire case to the jury. I was still in America wasn't I?

I would follow Renee to Federal Court to see what could be done about this. These Judges had stepped way over the line! I held my ground and angrily asked her if she liked to play naked games with little kids? She looked a little horrified but she just kept repeating "it is so ordered, it is so ordered" as if she was some type of God. This woman was sitting up there in her black robe doing the bidding of the Devil and I was supposed to take her seriously? Qadira wasn't her daughter! Scott hadn't done anything to her yet she was making it her business to protect this scumbag.

All the lies he had told me, all the bullshit he had put my family through, and I wasn't even going to be able to present my case to a jury because if I did I would win and win big. God forbid we would ever get any of these people's money. They just had to make sure that never happened. Their money was God. More sacred than life or duty to country. They loved the money. The money had to be protected at all costs.

The sound of my blood boiling was echoing in my ears and after letting her know that I knew what she was up to I found myself storming out of the courtroom. I was going to have to file another complaint, and this time on Judge Nelson for trying to cover up the abuse of my daughter. And not long after that the federal court threw out Renee's case against the judges who had presided over the case against Nike in the state. No opinion, no explanation, no nothing. It was always the same response. SLAP, KICK, PUNCH! These people answered to no one.

The school year was fast upon us and we decided due to Qadira's new diagnosis that we wanted her close to home. We transferred her back to Grey Middle School which was our neighborhood school. We wrestled with the decision because the all-girls school had done wonders for her but coping with her new diagnosis of diabetes was a lot. The school bus stopped just right outside our back steps where the picture of her bloody leg still hung. She begged us to remove the sign and we finally gave in. Nobody cared anyway and it was killing her social life. Even her old group of friends from Hayhurst kind of shunned her when she moved back to Grey, but no one really bothered her about it because they knew it had happened. Qadira had a way about her. She held her head up high and focused on her Japanese lessons. She always did a good job of trying to make the best of things.

And now Renee was working as a security guard at Wells Fargo in Downtown Portland and had a front row seat to the rise of Occupy Portland. We tried to take our concerns to a group of people whom we thought would be sympathetic to our plight, but once again we were kicked to the ground. SLAP, KICK, PUNCH! One night on their Facebook page as I tried to raise awareness as to what we were up against a bunch of people started ganging up on me, calling me names, and beating me down to the ground. They called me a "circle jerk" and a "bitch" and every other name in the book. They wanted to know what an "al Qadira" was. Who were these people?

It was brutal shameless attack and I knew the movement was being led by phonies and fakes. I wondered if people knew what they had gotten themselves into. When I attended one of their general assembly's I was suspicious of the guy in the red coat and the girl in the red hat that seemed to be running everything. While I was there they especially asked for woman to get up and speak but when I got on the microphone and started to get the crowd pumped up I was asked to leave. They shut Renee down as well. This wasn't a real movement. It was a bought and paid for show to help quell the revolutionary sentiment brewing up in America. The blind were leading the blind right off a cliff.

And the drama continued when in late November Qadira fractured her right leg. The poor girl couldn't get a break. It turned out that the burn had done way more damage than we could have ever suspected. Thanks to our newly adopted dog Roger whose lust for balls had directed him to haphazardly ram into Qadira at the dog park; the truth was pouring out all over the place.

Her leg had literally just snapped in half. Another trip to the hospital and my suspicions were raised when Joshua, Kamaya's old nurse came into Qadira's room to examine her X-ray's. I remembered him for his flamboyant personality when Kamaya had been a patient at the hospital, but unable to recall who he was at the moment of his appearance I ended up questioning the nurse he had come in with after he had left. "Hey wasn't that the guy that calls himself the baby healer" I asked. "Oh, Joshua" she replied. "Yes he treated my other daughter a few years ago" I said. "Oh yes he usually works in Oncology" she stuttered "I mean um ah I meant infectious disease." Why was this woman stuttering? And didn't oncology mean cancer? Suddenly I was suspicious again. Were Qadira's doctors hiding something more from us? I didn't question the nurse any further. What was the point? But I told myself I would get to the bottom of all of this.

So in between trying to take care of everything else we were moving a hospital bed into our house. Qadira's recovery was going to take some time which meant we were going have to pull her out of school for a while. Unable to get a good handle on her blood sugars at the hospital they began to fast track her to an insulin pump. Normally she would have had to endure one full year on needles before getting the pump but for her they were going to make an exception. That was the good news.

She now had a long dark scar on her right leg where they had cut her open to add 4 titanium screws to repair what had been broken. Her regular bed now sat too low to the floor for her to get in and out of so I borrowed an old hospital bed from Benchview, that way Qadira could have more control. The first few days were tricky but we managed to get through it. But I could still hear that nurse stuttering in the back of my head and first chance I got I intended to take Qadira back to the doctor for more tests. I was so tired of being lied to and so worried about my daughter's health. It always seemed we never had a chance to come up for air.

So as the days passed by I spent as much time as I could with her when I wasn't at work. We watched a lot of old episodes of the Twilight Zone to pass the time. We all now felt like we had a permanent address there. Everything was so surreal. It was very hard going through the motions every single day but somehow we managed to keep up appearances. This was all in an effort to keep our family together and our kids smiling. Failure was not an option. I wish I could say things were always sunny at our house but the fight was taking a tremendous toll on everyone.

You must at this point be wondering how we even managed to interact with our 3 other children or work or do much of anything and all I can tell you is that it is one giant blur but somehow we did it. For the everyday mundane things there was autopilot and when the pressure was too much there was the liquor store. Wading through the river of shit was all we ever did anymore. We didn't know anything else. Soon enough Christmas was upon us again and we were fast into 2012. I must admit I was pretty upset when the world didn't end but hardly surprised. That would be my luck after all.

The trial against Vangelisti Kocher was set for January 17th and 18th 2012 at the Multnomah County Courthouse although we couldn't figure out what for. My complaint against Judge Nelson had been quickly dismissed and on January 13th she had granted with no explanation or opinion Callahan's motion to limit me from talking about anything that I had experienced during Vangelisti Kocher's representation of Qadira. I was basically supposed to show up to the courtroom and not say a word. If I opened my mouth about anything relevant to the case I would be held in contempt of court and arrested right there on the spot. I wasn't about to attend that circus.

It was pretty clear I had made more enemies then friends during this ordeal. And of course to add insult to injury guess who was on the witness list to testify on behalf of Vangelisti Kocher? None other than Todd Burkholder and Aimee McQuiston. What the fuck! Can you even believe that? First Scott pretends for months to be our daughter's attorney and then he has the audacity to call up the people he did the pretending for so they can come to his rescue? SLAP, KICK, PUNCH! I was just so done in so many ways with these people and their tactics. I emailed all the parties to let them know I wouldn't be attending the trial because I don't engage in covering up crimes.

This whole bullshit process had gotten to be so unbearable. If it wasn't for the actual real costs associated with Qadira's injuries maybe we could have just walked away but here she was saddled for life with all kinds of medical problems. She was going to need some type of compensation. At least a little something to help make her journey through life easier but without a fair process we couldn't even get her that.

I decided to file suit against Judge Nelson and all of the other judges involved in covering up the abuse of Qadira once again trying to follow in my husband's footsteps with little to no chance of success. They had thrown his case against the judges out and soon they would throw out mine but we wrote it up and filed it anyway. And then out of nowhere the bomb dropped.

THE BLOOD TESTS

There they were in black and white tucked away in Scott Kocher's files. A file we had somehow overlooked all this time. What was this man doing running around with my daughter's blood work? What did the tests mean? They had been ordered by OHSU yet sent out to a lab at Kaiser. Why? OHSU had their labs. When Renee started cross referencing the numbers that looked funny our minds were blown all over again. Back in 2008 the blood tests had revealed a shocking truth. SLAP, KICK, PUNCH and SLAP again!

Qadira had obviously been slowly dying. The failure to treat her burn had produced horrific results. The damage was extensive. Now we were beginning to see the whole picture. The burn had been a massive assault on her tiny little body. No wonder she had developed the Type 1 Diabetes. It was a miracle that she was even alive. Only God could have saved her because there was no other way she could have survived. At that time she was the walking dead. A ghost.

The tests revealed severe internal distress and a serious case of sepsis which is blood poisoning. That explained the mottled patchy skin that had plagued her leg for so long after the burn. It was a sure sign. They hadn't even been giving her any kind of antibiotic when she was thrown out of the hospital. She never had a chance and they knew it. The blood tests told the whole lurid tale. And all they had told me at the time was that she didn't have Kawasaki's disease and sent her home to die just because they could. We had been lied to repeatedly and now the proof was staring us in the face. Cold hard proof that felt like the biggest back hand someone could deliver. SLAP, KICK, PUNCH! It was immobilizing.

We called the police and the FBI with news of what had to be the "smoking gun" but once again they argued with us and hung up on us. "It was insanity! Renee lay in the bed for several days just saying that he couldn't do it anymore. We tried to put in a report to the Inspector General but they refused to investigate. We were coming to terms with the fact that our government was rotten to the core. The smell of sulfer was everywhere.

We pulled our kids out of school and shut all of our shades not knowing what to do. Our world was forever changed. Kamaya's teacher called us begging us "not to give them a reason." A reason for what?

Was she insinuating that they would come and take our children away now, on top of everything else? Of course we knew at some point we needed to send the kids back to school but we just needed to take a moment and think. What little bit of sanity we had thought existed was all the way gone. The missing link had been found and it was terribly ugly. Now the whole thing was so obvious.

THE TRUTH

The President of OHSU Joe Robertson was good friends with
Rex Burkholder so it was easy to see how they arranged for Qadira to
be tossed out of the hospital and left to die. Now it was becoming
clear where the disputed information in her medical records had
come from. It had been easy to keep Providence on board since they
were already in on it after trying to buy Rex some time by failing to
call the police and failing to properly treat Qadira on the night of
April 12th 2007.

Dr. Julie Andrews made sure to give us no direction that night so
there had been a good chance that we would fail to bring Qadira back
to the hospital. It was now so obvious because when we showed up
at OHSU the next day they used the same tactic.

Nobody considered Qadira to be as valuable as Rex. If she had
died in our care in the following days the State could have just put
the blame squarely back on us saying we should have known better
and brought her back to the hospital. They would have charged us
with child abuse and failure to seek medical treatment, taken away
our children, and had us arrested. Of course with Qadira dead we
wouldn't have had the presence of mind to ask questions or fight
anything. But to the chagrin of many Qadira continued to against all
odds get up and live.

So now it was becoming utterly apparent why Phil Knight had
given OHSU 100 million dollars on October 29th 2008. This had
after all been the exact same day that the Portland Police had

definitively chosen to close Qadira's case. What are the odds of that? I had the letter staring me in the face. It was a little piece of information that had been uncovered long after the trial in my quest to get Qadira an investigation. All we had to do was look at what the police would have uncovered if they had gone looking into things. The blood tests were shockingly undeniable. Qadira was as good as dead. Initially Scott had hid that information to protect the hospitals and his friend Rex, but after Renee filed suit in 2008, Nike in a fit of uncontrollable rage had jumped on the bandwagon. He was a hair up their ass and they wanted to see him punished for what he had done.

They never had any intention of ever shutting Exeter down when they launched their so-called strategic review after firing Renee in 2007. It had all been one big show. They had fully expected due to our limited financial circumstances for Renee to just sign the severance agreement and go away.

This would have absolved them of the initial EEOC charge and they would be rid of someone whom they considered nothing but a big problem. But instead of a signed severance agreement they got two more EEOC charges and a lawsuit. To say they were a little pissed off is putting it mildly. They wanted to make Renee pay big for what he had done. In fact they were itching to jump on the bandwagon by the time it rolled by.

Suddenly they were presented with the opportunity to help Rex, Joe, Scott, Richard, and Rudy to drive us insane. Hell yeah, why not? If they could get Renee and me to act out in a violent manner all of their newfound troubles would go away instantaneously almost like magic. It was a win-win situation for everyone involved. No wonder the trial had been so bizarre. It had been specifically designed to drive us insane.

Todd and Aimee being absolved of all responsibility coupled with Qadira getting absolutely nothing after a massive beat down in the courtroom should have done the trick. Human behavior is usually pretty predictable and in all fairness they probably had a 99.9 percent chance of success. Most people would have snapped under the pressure because it was that heavy. With Renee finally out of the picture Nike could stop hiding Exeter and get the business up and running again and after all the trouble they felt he had caused them they were quite pleased with the circumstance and the opportunity for revenge.

JUSTICE FOR QADIRA

They couldn't believe it when they didn't get the desired results that they had hoped for from the trial. They had thrown everything and the kitchen sink into that trial and all it had done was cause more problems. Now things were even worse because now not only were we running all over town alerting anyone and everyone to what happened but the lawsuit hadn't gone away. They couldn't resume normal operations at Exeter with all that going on. And of course to everyone's growing exasperation Qadira kept getting up and living.

It was starting to spook people out. Qadira should be dead. It had been the hospitals prediction that she would die just days after the injury but after the trial it was now more than 16 months after the fact. It was becoming terribly anxiety producing for OHSU every single time we brought Qadira to the doctor. Not only was she the "walking dead" but the web of lies they were being forced to maintain grew larger day by day. Qadira's sudden mysterious death would have certainly devastated our family and solved a whole host of issues for a whole lot of people. But it just wasn't happening.

And making absolutely sure that the police did not investigate and uncover this information was paramount on everyone's mind. If the blood tests ever came to light a whole lot of people would be in trouble and Qadira might live. If that happened they would be punished instead of us. Nobody wanted that. But the price tag for this operation was going to be very high. Qadira had already miraculously survived much longer than any of the doctors had anticipated and people were getting very nervous. Sepsis is usually pretty fatal even when aggressively treated. OHSU was faced with continuing to lie to us for an unknown period of time. It could be months, it could be years. Keeping up the facade was going to be a lot of work. Donating the money to OHSU was a very sly way to reward them for a job well done and pay off the state to ensure its continued cooperation. People had 100 million reasons to get on board.

The Phil Knight Cancer institute in exchange for continuing to lie to us about Qadira's health was just one life for many. It was a small sacrifice in the big scheme of things. Why not? According to the blood tests she had very little time left. It all made sense now. Now I understood why Lachenmeier and Scott just kept telling us to spend some time with our daughter. That had been there guilty conscience talking out loud. OHSU was in charge of all her medical care at the time so they were holding all of the cards. We trusted them. With careers on the line and nobody wanting to go down for what had happened to Qadira, Phil Knight suddenly emerged in a fit of rage just waving fistfuls of cash around.

Nike had greatly reduced operations and attempted to hide a very lucrative business to deflect the EEOC charges after Renee had complained. He had cost them tons and tons of money. Making sure Qadira died was the perfect revenge. No one had to actually lay a hand on her to kill her but no one had to help her either. All her doctors had to do was keep lying to us and the infection was set to take care of the rest.

Whenever we brought her in with an issue it was always no big deal: a cold, flu, anxiety. They had all continued to pretend that the burn was no big deal. You have to be in bed with a special kind of evil to do something like this. Straight to our face they had lied and lied and lied. It was a miracle that she had survived and was doing so well. I knew in my heart that if we had given up fighting for her we would have lost her.

I found myself feeling grateful that I had chosen to fight Vangelisti Kocher. Sure I hadn't won any Money but I do believe Qadira's life was a much better prize. I am and continue to be eternally grateful that my growing mistrust of OHSU had led us to take Qadira to Emanuel the day she almost died. In Hebrew Emanuel means "God is with us" and God had certainly been with us that day and each and every day since Qadira was burned. We were certain that had we brought Qadira to OHSU when the diabetes threatened to overwhelm her they would have just sent her home to die. They had their marching orders from the money. We were very blessed that she had ever so conveniently gotten sick on a holiday weekend and slid in under the wire undetected by her predators.

We needed answers to burning questions and it was time to call everyone out. We wrote a scathing 68 page federal lawsuit and filed it in the District Court against all of the involved parties. It included a very long list of individuals and institutions. We made sure to include Phil Knight personally as well as Nike. It was our attempt to alert everyone we could to what had happened. At this point we weren't sure who knew what but we knew everybody knew something. A whole lot of people had come together to cover up the abuse of Qadira and we wanted to know why?

When it came time to serve the suit even Attorney General Eric Holder got a copy. The Federal Marshall delivered copies everywhere. We put the whole government on notice. If the police and FBI were going to ignore us at least they could do so with a paper trail following them around. Certainly with this new bit of information our right to a jury trial should have been secure. It was our constitutional right. But we were prepared for them to throw us out because that's all they had ever done. Slap us in the face and throw us to the ground. SLAP, KICK, PUNCH! It was the same tactic employed over and over and over to drive us completely insane. Obviously these people wanted us to kill ourselves or someone else.

We were scared to death of our own government and we filed that complaint for our own protection. Somewhere a report of what happened must be generated and they were not going to let us file one. There had to be some kind of paper trail if something happened to us. We were dropping breadcrumbs in case we suddenly disappeared. Unable to use the system we found a way in through the back door.

Renee quit his job doing security because we now feared for our lives and ABM had asked him to go through an open shooter program. It was very scary to be doing all of this alone. We were acutely aware that we knew too much and we had stepped on a lot of big toes. Three times after we filed the big complaint Renee found the bolts on the wheels of our van unscrewed. It was very nerve racking. Since we were not allowed to file any police reports about anything we kept our mouths shut and tried to look out for ourselves.

We painstakingly reviewed everything that had happened carefully putting all of the facts and evidence together while reeling at what we had discovered. It was terrifying. We alerted the kid's teachers and principals to what was going on. We transferred Qadira back to the all-girls school after the principal of Grey middle school was rude and dismissive of our plight. We worried about the kids whenever they were out of our sight and we sought protection wherever we could get it by making as many regular people as we could aware of our situation and gauging their response.

I took Qadira to see a new doctor at the Nara clinic but she was obviously in on it as well. We were nothing but trouble and the whole town seemed to be on notice. We didn't make a move they didn't see. Dr. Amy Earhart played just as dumb as the rest of them or maybe even dumber but I wasn't taking it lying down. I told her everything about Qadira's untreated burn and I alerted her diabetic doctor as well. You should have seen the look on their faces. I demanded that they run full metabolic blood tests on Qadira and I requested that I receive a copy of those tests. I had lost all trust for any kind of authority. I needed to be sure of what was going on with my daughter's health.

I wanted to compare those tests to the ones that had been taken in 2008. I wasn't about to trust these people with my daughter anymore. When the tests came back and I was able to do a comparison I was relieved to see that her body was no longer under distress. Her liver still looked a little out of whack and her vitamin D levels came in lower than that of children in 3rd world countries but other than that it looked like after the diabetes scare a lot of issues had been corrected. Her white blood cell count was now normal and the massive infection was gone. Emanuel hospital must have been taking a lot heat for doing that.

All the research I had done on burns was serving me well. Now I demanded a bone density scan (DEXA) of her bones from her endocrinologist. I knew that in 2004 vitamin D supplementation had become mandatory in burned children due to a high incidence of osteopenia in burn victims. Qadira's leg had just snapped in two when Roger hit her. Renee and Kymani didn't even believe she was really hurt at first because it didn't seem like the impact should have hurt her that badly much less broken her leg. I remembered Joshua coming into her room and the nurse mentioning oncology. Was there something wrong with her bones I wondered?

When we got the results of the DEXA scan it was more bad news. She was now diagnosed with Osteopenia and Scoliosis. The images on the screen had horrified Renee. She looked all crooked on the inside. Her body had been working overtime to repair the damage from the burn and she had suffered irreparable damage throughout all that. And the doctors continued to stand around and play dumb. Dr. Earhart just wanted to know why I ordered the DEXA showing zero concern for the diagnosis.

I wanted to smack the shit out of her, but I kept my cool. This dumb broad hadn't even called me to talk about Qadira's recent blood tests and then after I brought them up sat there repeatedly insisting that Qadira's vitamin D levels were just super low because we lived in Oregon. Then she had the audacity to refer Qadira back to OHSU for treatment. My blood just boiled away in my ears. Every official we encountered was a psychopath. It was pure insanity!

We frantically tried to find a different primary provider but nobody would take us. We eventually resigned ourselves to just bossing Dr. Earhart around. It was her choice to keep acting like an idiot. The next order of business was an MRI of the burned leg and another diagnosis. She had Kissing Contusions (bone bruises) that were hidden beneath the long dark scar. Now we understood why her left leg would snap out of place from time to time causing her to just fall to the ground. SLAP, KICK, PUNCH over and over and over. Blood was everywhere. And In the middle of all this we were still trying to live our lives. I was still caregiving and Renee had begun honing his skills as a carpenter taking every odd job that he could find to help keep our heads above water.

We really felt that Qadira needed a work up by someone who could troubleshoot this thing from the very beginning. I contacted Marc Jeske a burn doctor and researcher who used to work for Shriners Burn Center in Galveston, Texas which is considered to be one of the best burn centers in the world. He told me Qadira should be seen at the Burn Center right away. I contacted Shriners and explained the situation and sent them information but once again they refused to see Qadira. In fact Dr. Hernandez was pretty damn rude.

One of the things we had hoped to achieve by filing the 68 page lawsuit was to secure proper medical care for our daughter. We were asking for a grand jury investigation and for protection for our family but the answer was always a cold hard slap in the face. SLAP, KICK, PUNCH! In regards to the lawsuit there was nothing but silence. We couldn't even find anyone to treat her osteopenia so it was going to have to go untreated for now. Apparently OHSU was the only hospital in town that could do it but we were afraid to let any of their doctors anywhere near our daughter.

By this time I was really beginning to search for answers in the scripture. After visiting several churches and the local mosque searching for some kind of help and finding none I began to read as much scripture as I could in my very limited free time. We were all alone in this and I searched diligently for meaning. For a while I even cut Haley off completely. It was maddening how nobody understood and sometimes I could not bear to be around people. My family life and job were totally overwhelming. I began pouring over scripture looking for answers.

I had never owned a copy of the Quran but one day we decided to visit the local mosque looking for help. The men at the front door refused to invite us both in through the front door to talk. We were told women must go around through the back door and only converse with other woman. That was not going to work for either of us. We were in this together. I wasn't about to go in anybody's back door after everything I had been put through and my husband would never ask me to do something like that. We were equals. So we explained the situation at the front door and of course nobody offered to help us but someone named Ahmed didn't want us to leave empty handed so he gave us a copy of the book. I had gone to Bible study as a child but was totally unfamiliar with the Quran and so was Renee who had been raised Catholic. I have to say it turned out to be a pretty interesting read.

My favorite passages in the book were the ones that talked about the messengers and the scalding water. It said the messengers would throw the scalding water in the faces of their enemies and make them taste their bad deeds. Sounded familiar to me; I also liked the passages that talked about the criminals arguing in the fire as they blamed one another for their bad decisions. I wasn't interested in becoming a Muslim but the book certainly caught my attention. And in the Bible it was the Book of Job and the Book of Revelations that held me captive. When I finally had a chance to watch the Passion of the Christ I was mesmerized. I had to watch it twice. Jesus was definitely somebody I could not help but have a deep admiration for. Over the next few weeks and months I kept both books close by my side.

Renee's race discrimination suit and the "big lawsuit" and my lawsuit against the judges now all sat before Federal judge Michael W. Mosman. He proclaimed to be a member of the Mormon Church so I was faced with reading yet another book. I ordered a copy of the Book of Mormon trying to see if it could help me understand how to appeal to this man's morality if he really even had any. We had been thrown out of court so many times and I was trying to determine if this guy had any kind of backbone. It seemed to me that most people just followed the money but I was always willing to give someone the benefit of the doubt.

The book was nothing like the Quran which was easy to read because it read more like poetry. This book reminded me more of the Bible kind of hard to decipher because of the flowery language but in the end I felt like all three books were essentially the same. Totally and completely disrespected and misunderstood by the people that read them. I even believed this about the Baha'i scriptures I had laying around from when I had been heavily involved in that religion as a teenager. And even Self Realization Fellowship the church founded by Paramahansa Yogananda that Renee and I had joined together shortly before we married was bought and paid for. Not the teachings of course but the people who were involved. It was all just big business down here. And who could blame them? It was all about the money down here.

As a matter of fact as things had spiraled totally out of control for us after Renee lost his job at Nike a monk at SRF had basically told him to give up. What was that all about? Just because someone says they know and trust God doesn't really mean much with all the money to be made off of religion nowadays. I imagined poor Jesus and Muhammad and other great religious leaders rolling around in their graves in horror as they were bought and sold on the market place to the highest bidder.

The silence from the Federal Court was so loud and Qadira's medical problems so pressing and I was supposed to be living in a country that was founded on values and laws? But the only thing that anyone seemed to really value was money. Nobody had come to our aid. Every single person in our lives had told us to give up. Not even one person including my own family members had even bothered to write one letter or make one phone call on behalf of Qadira or Renee. Everyone was just too busy chasing the money and could I blame them? They were being told they needed it to survive. Helping our family would be taking a huge risk. What if they lost their money too? You could die in this place without it. It was literally that serious.

I was determined to make Mosman notice us and I declared in one of our response briefs that we were indeed "The Messengers." I had certainly begun to feel that way. What else could we be? How else could all of this stuff have happened to us yet we were against all odds still standing. I quoted the Bible, the Book of Mormon, and the Quran. I had given up on the law because I could see quite plainly that there was none. Renee chose to stay more technical in his fight against Nike but he too began to deviate from our more standard protocol. I wasn't even surprised when Mosman threw out my case against the judges. He was bought and paid for. I appealed the decision to the Ninth Circuit court of appeals and they threw that out to. SLAP, KICK, PUNCH! No opinion. No explanation. Just get out. This wasn't America. This was Nazi Germany. We had no rights at all.

And when Nike asked to depose Renee once again we didn't bother to prepare. They were the ones who had something to hide. When we walked into the Federal Courthouse that day where a room was being provided for the deposition I carried all 3 books with me. When Amy Joseph Pederson tried to give me attitude I blew fire in her direction. She no longer intimidated me. I was going to leave the room when I was good and ready not on her command. She was doing the Devil's work. I handed Renee the Quran and said to him "take this; it will be a light for you in dark places." He hadn't read a word of the book but I just gave it to him so that he wouldn't have to go into another battle empty handed.

This was nothing but another show to try and kick us down some more. SLAP, KICK, PUNCH! They loved beating us and slapping us and laughing at us behind closed doors. They had enough money to pay for the decisions they wanted rendered. We didn't have a chance. Our rights did not exist. We were not nearly as valuable as their master. Phil Knight owns Oregon. And in a way Nike owned the United States. No one wanted to see them go down. What would we all do when the Olympics rolled around? We were a dirty little secret to be shoved into the closet and left to rot. They were just waiting for the perpetual poverty, depression, and virtual media blackout to drive us mad. Even though we really won each case we still lost.

They were determined that we would suffer and making sure we didn't get our hands on any money was a major part of the plan. They would string us along and then slap us down as hard as they could every chance they got. It was frustrating for them because we were now too entrenched in our community for us to suddenly up and disappear. That would not look good at all. Lots of suspicion would be raised if we all suddenly ended up dead and it would all point back to them. Our friends and family and too many people in the wealthy Jewish community we lived in would be asking questions. Nobody wanted anybody asking "What happened to the Stephens family." The strategy was just to keep bearing down hard until we did ourselves in. It was a unified front.

We kept fighting. Court brief after court brief we tried our best to get them to see what they were doing was wrong but they showed no mercy. On April 12th 2012 in a last ditch effort to try and recoup Qadira's losses we filed another lawsuit in the State Court just against Providence and OHSU. We had named them in the big lawsuit as well but we were not sure if that was the right venue or not. We both felt strongly that the hospitals were particularly responsible. They were the ones that should have put their feet down in the first place when they saw the damage to Qadira. They should have had the presence of mind to tell Rex that they just couldn't cover up what had happened. If the hospitals had just followed their own protocol the mess the burn produced would have been drastically smaller. Sure Todd and Aimee would have been charged and sentenced but that would have been the end of it. We reasoned that surely someone would be prepared to hold them accountable once they fully understood the magnitude of what they had truly done.

Shortly thereafter the all-girls school Qadira was attending was suddenly shut down. SLAP, KICK, PUNCH. By the years end we would have to find a new school for her to attend. The timing seemed a little fishy but we were used to rolling with the punches. It was another big change. But by this time things for Qadira were looking up. She was now after only two short years fairly fluent in Japanese and much to the growing irritation of those who wished to harm her she landed a spot in Mt. Tabor's Japanese immersion program. Qadira like her father was well liked by everyone who met her.

We contacted more attorneys, more police officers and tried our hardest to continue to elevate and at the same time keep a tight eye on Qadira's health. We made flyers that had a picture of the Nike "swoosh + OHSU = child abuse" and plastered it all over our own neighborhood, downtown, and all the way around the outside of the Nike campus and up and down the road leading to OHSU. They took them down as fast as we could put them up. We started going down to Pioneer Square speaking about what we had experienced in the courts, trying to alert people to the corrupt leadership, but people could not seem to grasp the magnitude of what we were saying. Once again we got tuned out.

The media had done a good job of hiding us and nobody knew who we were or what we were up to. In regards to what we referred to as the "big lawsuit" the motions to dismiss poured in from attorneys' all over town. All the parties answered admitting to what they had done yet asking the court to just dismiss us anyway which is exactly what Mosman did on July 13 2012. He based his very short opinion on the "alleged burn" (despite the fact that we had proved that it had occurred) and he made sure to point out that he could have fined us over 70,000 dollars for complaining. He slapped a pre-filing order on both of us making filing anymore lawsuits of any kind contingent on the courts approval. He offered no real explanation of anything. SLAP, KICK, PUNCH!!! Blow after blow they bloodied us with their abuse of power. We weren't even allowed one hearing before we were thrown out. We filed an appeal with the Ninth Circuit Court of Appeals along with all the evidence we had to support our claims and we waited.

The kids were all doing surprisingly well despite all of this. All four of them even joined us for one of our protests. Even though we never went to church Qayden became a staunch believer in God frequently exclaiming "They are not going to win, right dad?" He would say it with all earnestly "Because they don't have God on their side." He began to make this declaration all of the time. I sure hoped he was right. The welfare juggling act, my terribly hard caregiving job and Renee's daily scramble to keep some money coming in from his carpentry gigs was just stress upon stress. That coupled with all of the legal work was so utterly exhausting and we were broke all of the time. It never seemed to end but somehow we had to keep fighting.

Whatever fake court decisions were thrown at us we knew we had to keep up the work or face even more dire consequences. We were certain that if we hadn't kept fighting we would have lost Qadira. There was just no other way for us to go. And on September 17th we knew we were going to continue getting the smack down because there was Phil and Penny Knight raining what I like to call "fuck you" money down on the State. OHSU received its largest gift ever of 125 million dollars. There was just no way we could compete with all that money but we kept trying anyway. What did the law matter in the face of such wealth? Phil was a God to the people of The United States of America and they bowed down to him and his money.

So on October 30th we were called to a hearing in front of Judge Skye down at the Multnomah County Courthouse. The hospitals had filed their motions to dismiss and we weren't expecting any kind of justice. But we brought Qadira with us so they would have to at the very least tell her to her face that they thought she didn't matter and that she deserved nothing. And it wasn't long before Judge Skye started in with her bullshit. She wasn't even going to let Qadira say anything when I asked if she could speak.

I squared up my shoulders and I told that woman that at the very least she was going to let my daughter speak. She shut her mouth for a few seconds and Qadira very politely looked at her and said "ever since I was burned, ever since this happened my parents have been trying to get help and no one is helping them…" Judge Skye looked distressed trying to counter with what is legal and what is not but the three of us knew better. Her job was to protect the money.

In the middle of her speech Renee cut in "I am sorry he said, but I am leaving." He was fed up and I tried to get him to sit back down but he turned on Judge Skye "This isn't a courtroom" he said "This is a circus, and you're not a judge, you're a clown." He angrily left the room. She finished her blah, blah, blah and it was over.

We were all just so exhausted. They just called us down to the courthouse to slap us around some more. SLAP, KICK, PUNCH! God forbid Qadira would be compensated for her injury. It was serve and protect the money at all costs no matter how wrong they knew they were. It was positively, mind numbingly disgusting how they bowed down to the Almighty Dollar. What the fuck had come over all these people? Qadira was just a little girl and her injuries were real. We filed another appeal begging the court to value life but it was denied.

On November 14th Renee got a bullhorn and tried to get people to follow him down to the courthouse where Judge Mosman was going to be presiding over his summary judgment hearing in regard to his race discrimination lawsuit against Nike. We knew an empty courtroom was a sure death sentence and we wanted people to see how the so called judges just disregarded the law with impunity but once again nobody seemed to care at all. Only a handful of homeless people, our kids, and my mom and Sala showed up in the courtroom. Mosman did Nike's bidding leaving all of the material facts at issue and tossing the case out. No real opinion, explanation, no nothing. When we left the courtroom the clerk raced after Renee with the copy of the Bible that he had brought with him.

She said "Sir, sir, you need to take your things." He turned around and he said "That's the Bible." To which she replied "Sir, I know but you have to take your things." To which he replied sternly "I am leaving that for the Devil." She looked horrified. She followed us outside where Qayden proceeded to climb up on some stairs and scramble up on a concrete ledge and jump. She followed us out asking him not to do that for his own safety. Like she actually cared about my son's safety?

I grabbed his arm and stared her straight in the eyes "come honey" I said "It stinks of sulfur around here." I was done. And with that we walked away from the system for good; me, my son, my husband, and our entire family. We didn't want any of their stupid fucking money. What we wanted was for someone to care. There was no going back. Our fate was sealed. Renee filed another appeal with the Ninth Circuit but we didn't really expect to hear back from them. It was time to change the world.

And on December 14 2012 after Adam Lanza gunned down 20 children in a horrific massacre that was plastered all over the news we were finally visited by the so called authorities. It was an officer Dale Haskins and a black suit without a name. They came to our house looking for my husband while I was pulling into our gravel driveway after work. I had all my things in my hands as I exited the car but in a deep show of exasperation I planted my things on the hood of my vehicle and said "what's up?" Dale asked me "Is your husband planning something?" What the hell? Had he not read our lawsuit? Was my husband planning something? What about all the plans that had been made behind our backs? I told them that they could come back tomorrow and that they could talk to Renee in person.

And they came back the next morning and we were both home to greet them. They came in as if they were coming to have tea and cookies and asked if we were planning on committing a "Mass Shooting?" What the fuck was the matter with these people? After everything that had happened and they were concerned about our behavior? You have got to be kidding me!

There we all were talking about how a bunch of insane officials had tortured and tried to kill our daughter, and how unsafe we felt, and suddenly they were asking us if we were planning on committing a mass shooting? And when we firmly told them absolutely not, then they just wanted to know if we were going to hurt Phil.

We told them our whole story and still at the end they just wanted to know if we were going to try to hurt Phil? Our story, what he tried to do to us and what he had done to Qadira was of no consequence to them. We were nobody and every chance they got they told us that. The no name FBI agent shook Renee's hand and told him that he sincerely hoped we got justice for our daughter.

PAY IT FORWARD LEADERSHIP SOCIETY

Now we were totally awake and everything was terribly distressing to watch; families of veterans losing lives fighting for a freedom that had long ago been bought and sold to the highest bidder. Homeless people dying in the streets as banks and fat cats laughed shamelessly. A booming sex slave trade and millions of broken people locked up in tiny cages and war, war, and more war. There was blood all over the walls; people everywhere just swimming in oceans of blood. Killing everywhere as far as the eye could see, all the life on the planet being killed with impunity. It was so disgusting, so distressing!

Naked, starving real people as far as the eye could see and a bunch of elected officials who were no more than high paid actors pretending to care about people who were desperately depending on them to help them make sense of the very lives that they were trying to live. It was a horrific sight. Far worse than any horror movie we could have ever imagined. There was a river of filthy stinking shit flowing right through the middle of the world we had been born and raised in.

I expected nothing and wanted nothing. It would have been nice to have a reprieve from the poverty and the depression but even if we had won some of their beloved money it wouldn't be enough to solve the problems we were now facing. Our whole worldview had been destroyed and the message was beginning to take over every aspect of our lives. It had become very clear where the entire world's problems were stemming from.

Another Christmas and New Year's goes by with every single one of our so called elected officials ignoring our pleas for some help. They thought they would show us just how worthless we really were by treating us like we didn't exist at all. The only thing they cared about was the money. And we were just supposed to sit there and accept that while they sat comfortably in their positions of authority telling everyone what to do. We had watched them literally shit and piss all over their own system with no regard for who got hurt. It was all just fun and games to them. And they did it all for the money.

Renee began to walk the streets looking for answers. One day he pulled an 85 year old woman out of a sleeping bag on the streets of downtown Portland. She used to be a teacher but financial misfortune led to her demise and she was thrown away by society. There were so many people and they all had terrible stories to tell about how they had been cast out from society. There was no justice to be had in this world. More and more we began to realize that the reason our daughter had been treated so poorly was because nobody on the planet cared about life. And since money was the focus of their society how could they? Certainly the leadership had shown they had zero regard. We had literally begged them to care and we had gotten their answer: "Denied."

Virtually all of the life around us was either suffering terribly or disappearing at an alarming rate. It was so terrible. In this world the money was always afforded the first consideration, the last consideration and every single consideration in between. Human Beings had become totally disposable in the face of this new tyranny. We had gotten that message loud and clear. Renee got a white t-shirt and wrote on it in all capital letters "I AM A HUMAN BEING AND I MATTER, NOT MONEY!" and began to wear it all over town. Somehow we had to find a way to save as much of the life as we could.

In February of 2013 we officially founded The Pay It Forward Leadership Society determined to change the world. Renee used his experience from all of his years in design to develop our logo which we named "The circle" and "The seal" and we made our first official shirt. We felt we had identified a serious problem in our society that needed to be immediately addressed. We kept going down to Pioneer Square in the middle of downtown Portland to see if we could began to raise the awareness of the issue. Once again we thought that people would be alarmed at our discovery but like all the times before we got tuned out. We made speeches, passed out flyers, and set up a Facebook page and YouTube channel to promote our cause.

Our concern for our fellow man began to grow as more and more people from all walks of life complained that the real problem was that there were just too many people on the planet. What the fuck? We were horrified! How could so many people have come to believe that? Who did everyone think was going to help clean up this mess if everyone just wanted all the people gone? We were certain that if we could just get people to understand that it was the life that mattered then we could make the whole world a better place. We hoped to achieve a new understanding that without life there would be nothing.

We began to hear it over and over and over from everyone that "It's never going to happen!" But, why not? We began to question everyone, and anyone who would listen. We earnestly began to wonder why nobody wanted to matter. We asked people to get a white t-shirt and a black sharpie and write on it "I AM A HUMAN BEING AND I MATTER, NOT MONEY!" and join us down at the square. We envisioned a large group of people coming together to help communicate to the leadership that they were headed in the wrong direction but not one person showed up. We were totally perplexed. Could it be that people did not want to matter more than money?

The more time we spent in the shirts the more concerned we became. Even the people around us who knew what happened to us viewed us with annoyance and suspicion. Nobody could understand why we were so passionate about the cause because nobody could seem to wrap their minds around what we had been through. In our eyes there was no system. No matter how hard we tried to explain it our experience fell on deaf ears. We saw a population of people who were so well trained to believe in the system that they didn't even care if it worked anymore, and even in the face of its obvious failure, people were prepared to defend it at all costs. In the eyes of many once again we were the problem.

But by this time things in our life were starting to look just a little brighter. Our finances remained a total mess but Qadira managed to get a full scholarship to go to Japan realizing a big dream of hers. We made it perfectly clear to the school district that due to their involvement in the cover up that we did not trust them with our daughter and they paid for Renee to go with her. We were also able to refinance our house which once again saved our asses from foreclosure. Kamaya began to excel in the ballet classes gifted to her by her 3rd grade teacher and as always the boys chugged along. Qayden was becoming a very good student and Kymani had traded in his drawing pencil for the guitar. They all brought home good grades and remained on their best behavior for the most part. Things seemed to be looking up. Renee and I popped in and out of our shirts spending time when we could talk to people about the subject.

But we were still also reeling from the blows we had received and we had good days and bad days. The stress of being just over broke all the time was taking its toll. The Ninth Circuit had gone totally quiet and we began to realize that it was a real possibility that we would never hear from them. It was also a real possibility that our mission would fail.

We were always hoping that people would choose to act right but we had no idea how long it was going to take. We drank to relieve the pressure that seemed to always be building up in us. The more we talked to people the more we realized just how grave our circumstances truly were. We heard over and over and over from people of all walks of life that there was just "Too many people on the planet!" It was unbelievable how much people had stopped caring about each other. No wonder Renee had been cast out from his career and Qadira had almost been killed. Nobody wanted to take responsibility for anything down here. What was the point?

And the more we talked the more contempt we garnered for ourselves. After a while we stopped going down to the square because it was exhausting and it was utterly apparent that nobody cared. Even the people who pretended to care didn't really seem to care. After all no one we personally knew in our lives had ever bothered to pick up a phone or write a letter on behalf of Qadira or Renee so why should anyone support us now?

The further we fell the more the people around us seemed to revel in our demise. SLAP, KICK, PUNCH! Sure some people showed some concern to our faces when they heard our story but that was it. They were not going to support us in our mission. We tried to take it to the next level and made yet another shirt which said "I AM A LIVING BEING AND I MATTER, NOT MONEY!

We didn't know what it was going to take to get people to care but we were determined to try. And of course we were still trying to get some help for Qadira; still making phone calls, still contacting the police, and the mayor, and the media. But now we had definitely been shut out from society and we would not be accepted back. Go away they said to us. Go away and die.

But we kept getting up and going after it. Answers we needed answers! It was so aggravating!!! To watch all of our public officials just lying through their teeth as the bodies piled up in the streets. And everyone around us was just content to follow them around. We heard all the familiar cries of "Give up!" and "move on!" But give up and move on to where? There was nowhere to go.

One night in the summer of 2013 as I drowned my sorrows into another bottle of liquor I had a bad feeling. Where was Renee? Did he go to Todd's house I wondered in my fog? Suddenly I felt an urgency to go find him and I ran down the street. I knew where he was and I rounded the corner just in time to see him being handcuffed in front of Todd's house. I was screaming at the top of my lungs "HE IS TELLING THE TRUTH." Todd came out of his house and I had a few choice words for him. He tried to ask the officer to arrest me for disorderly conduct but I just turned on my heel and said "He isn't going to arrest anybody." I glared at the cop and went home to wait for Renee's call.

He had only gone over to talk to Todd and now they were arresting him? After all the bullshit we had been put through they arrested him. Oh my God! It just never ended up in here. When the kids found out what had happened Kymani only had two words for his dad "don't drop the soap" he advised him when he called home for a ride. Over the years he had turned into quite the little comic. Our kids had grown up making lemons out of lemonade. It was a kind of magic that made the darkness that surrounded us a little brighter.

And Renee hadn't given them an easy time down at the jailhouse yelling and screaming all night long about what they did to Qadira. They begged him to be quiet "Please sir we are just trying to get people processed." That's what he was told. And that's all there ever was. There was no justice. There was just a process. But it was so disturbing, so maddening, to see people getting put through a process that the leadership had absolutely no respect for. There were so many people who had gotten a "get out of jail" free card for helping to cover up the abuse of our daughter and the events at Nike. And there were just too many people who were simply "magically" allowed to avoid this potentially life destroying process that others had no means to escape. This wasn't anywhere near close to fair. How dare the leadership be doing this to people and how dare people not care!

And a few weeks later they did it again. SLAP, KICK, PUNCH, and "SLAP" again. Renee went out to Cactus Jacks which was a local bar, to order some to go food. While he was there he began discussing with some patrons some of our new ideas about getting rid of the use of money. And wouldn't you know it the bartender called the police on him. He wasn't loud or drunk and he hadn't even been talking to her. In fact, she hadn't even given him the food he paid for or let him finish his drink.

And here was the Portland Police arresting him again for no reason. Officer Sussman showed up and proceeded to tell Renee that he was "Satan" because he was trying to get people to believe what he believed. He informed him that he was a "Good slave" and that is what my husband needed to learn to be. They locked him up again for the whole night.

And Officer Sussman called me on the phone and told me he had arrested my husband for basically no reason. I had been super worried so I was so glad to hear he was okay. At this point it was like one in the morning and I really needed my car back. Cactus Jacks was a little bit of a hike from my house. I told him since he had arrested Renee for no reason then I would appreciate it if he came and gave me a ride and he actually came to my house and picked me up. I think he just wanted to talk. Maybe he was just trying to get a better grasp on the things that Renee was talking about. Maybe he was just trying to understand who we were but we talked until it was light outside. He even ended up showing me pictures of his family.

I think that secretly many of the officials we came into contact with were pretty disgusted at what had happened to us but they lacked the courage to really do anything about it. It was all about the money down here and they desperately needed their paychecks to survive. Renee showed back up after taking the bus back from downtown and he looked pissed. He hadn't bothered to call me because he thought I didn't have the car. They hadn't charged him, just wasted his time. The look on his face must have really spooked Officer Sussman because he left in a big hurry when he saw him coming our way.

It was not long after this that one day after Renee dropped me off at work that he had a feeling that he should go down to Pioneer Square by himself to speak. He didn't tell me what he was up to. He just dropped me off and headed downtown following a feeling that had begun to overwhelm him. When he arrived at the square he was surprised to find many local churches gathered together there at an event referred to as the International Praise Festival. It was a city wide event featuring culturally diverse Christian ministries within the Portland Metro area. What a great place to spread the message he thought to himself and he began talking to people.

He talked to as many individuals as he could about the fact that we as a race of Living Beings had replaced the value of life with money and everybody agreed with him. He thought that since everyone he talked to agreed with him that he would ask to speak to the crowd. He got on the stage and walked up to the man with the microphone and asked if he could address the crowd and immediately 3 men came and grabbed him and began to haul him away. He called out to the crowd "I have a message, by a show of hands who wants to hear me speak?" There was a loud silence as all the people he had just spoken to turned their backs on him and the three men dragged him to the sidewalk.

It was a unified front... They told him he was welcome to stay but he could see they didn't really mean it. He just decided to inform them that he had already given them the message and he left. All these people standing around pretending to praise God yet they couldn't make any time to discuss the fact that we as a race of beings had replaced the value of life with money? It was very frustrating!

The whole year through we popped in and out of our shirts trying to sound the alarm bell. Kamaya won a full scholarship so she could keep dancing. Turns out she was quite the talented little ballerina. There were silver linings everywhere and we did our best to keep our heads up. Things were still very ominous but better than they had been. We still hadn't gotten the reassurance that we had hoped for in regards to Qadira's health and we knew we were never going to get it. She was in God's hands and we were just thankful for every day that we got to keep her. And once again another Thanksgiving,

Christmas and New Year have passed us by. It seemed like time was speeding up, so much to do with so little time to get it all done. We kept on trying.

And 2014 brought with it more of a resolve to turn Pay It Forward into something real. Now instead of talking constantly about our court cases we moved into to talking about how to change the world. We printed up more shirts and did the t-shirt experiment whenever we could. Just walking around in the shirts got people talking but it was terribly exhausting. People are not used to other people openly questioning the money. And the more we talked to people the more we knew that somehow we had to get rid of the use of it.

It was a scourge on the entire planet but people were so incredibly blinded by its use, and it didn't even work for them. In fact it didn't work at all. It was an inanimate object that just sat in the way of everything that was good. And it was all the leadership cared about. It was always about saving the money. People, animals, and nature all disposable in the face of something that wasn't even real. How could we have done this to ourselves? Things were so bad that all one had to do was turn on the T.V to be assaulted by images of naked, starving, suffering people. It was horrible. This wasn't anywhere close to Heaven. It was Hell and we busied ourselves frantically looking for a way out.

And of course nobody cared because we are nobody. Without media coverage we were just like Frodo and Sam in the Lord of the Rings. And we knew that if we failed that all the life on the planet was doomed. We understood why our lives had been completely turned upside down and we were grateful. Someone had to busy themselves cleaning up this mess. We were just amazed at the reports the shirts were sending us. Humanity really just went ahead and replaced the value of life with money; totally and completely. They weren't just using the money. They believed in it. It was their God.

And they loved the money and they wanted to keep it more than anything else. And the very urgent calls for us to change the message started coming in from everywhere. People from all walks of life vehemently wanted us to stop attacking what they considered to be valuable. But it wasn't our message to change. There were days that we fielded so much bad energy from wearing the shirts that we couldn't wait to get home and take them off. Nobody cared about what happened to us and nobody wanted the message but we kept trying. And like our journey through the courts our words fell on deaf ears. Once again it was a unified front.

Our entire worldview had changed so drastically that we just could not imagine sending our children out into this filthy world. We found ourselves feeling very guilty that we had even brought them here. This was no way to experience life. Nobody deserved to live in a world that didn't care about them. We saw major world problems from a whole new perspective. It was so glaringly obvious what the real problem was. Our fellow Humans had taken their eyes so far off the ball that they could not find it anymore. In fact things had gotten so bad they didn't even want to talk about it. The truth was that our failure to provide for and check in on every single person on the planet had grown so large that now everybody just thought that getting rid of about 90 percent of the population was the answer; when you start hearing that from people of all walks of life it is terribly disturbing. And we were terribly disturbed.

And the world's religions were just big businesses selling God to whoever was buying. And people were buying left and right. The collection plates were overflowing. The snake oil salesman was on every single corner. It was so disgusting to watch. All these people claiming to believe in God yet here we stood as a race of beings slapping this so called God in the face as hard as we could. SLAP, KICK, PUNCH! Everywhere we looked there was death and destruction and a bunch of people standing around making excuses. More and more we could not understand why people begrudged one another access to society.

Why was there even a society being built and maintained if everyone was not going to be allowed to use it? It made no sense at all. There was so much stuff on the shelves at the stores but nobody was allowed to use any of it unless they had any money? Homes were built yet stood empty while real people were made to sleep out in the streets? Arguing, yelling, screaming and people just breaking other people left and right. And the children suffered the most just like Qadira had. Every time someone had a problem with someone else they tried to kill them. What the hell was going on down here? It was pure madness!

Our beloved society had no foundation. It had been built on a big old pile of paper. No wonder the whole place was going up in flames. It was all just lip service and fakery. The sound of our elected actors droned on in the background. Every single distraction they could think of to keep people from caring about one another was plastered all over the media. Our stomachs ached and churned as we realized the magnitude of the problem. There were people bitching and moaning that there wasn't enough to go around while tons of stuff was thrown in the garbage left and right.

And the only sense we could make out of the whole mess was the obvious. Humanity lived, worked, and died for money because that is what the so called leaders told them to do. It was pure madness! If our leaders did not care about life and they were leading everyone then it was imperative that people stop listening to them right away! As far as we were concerned the people in charge needed therapy and treatment not to be blindly followed around. And we tried our best to sound the alarm bell anyway we could. I ranted as loud as I could on Facebook and we began spending even more time in our shirts. But we just got tuned out.

People viewed us as stupid and judgmental. Just the statement coming from our mouths that life is what is valuable angered all of those around us. The more determined we got the angrier they got. It was so ridiculous what we were experiencing. Here we were in modern day America where Humanity had become so proficient that they could make a computer fit into a pocket yet they couldn't figure out how to take care of all of the life on the planet? And to make matters worse they didn't even want to try. In fact they didn't even want to talk about it. They just wanted to stand around arguing about problems that had simple solutions. It was pure insanity!

And in the middle of all of this we were still trying to live our lives. Qadira won a prestigious scholarship from the State Department to spend the summer in Korea. That girl always seemed to land on her feet. It was scary letting her go out into the world but her zest for life could not be contained. Kymani spent the summer working with Renee on odd jobs discovering that he also loved to work with his hands. Kamaya won a scholarship to a senior ballet intensive and Qayden began to emerge as a strong leader. Our kids were growing up and soon there would be no way to watch over them. We had to get this world cleaned up fast. And through all of this I began to realize that it wasn't enough to be in the t-shirts part time. We were going to have to start making this our full time job if we ever hoped to achieve anything. I sat Renee down and told him we must begin wearing the shirts all of the time. I was isolated at Benchview but he was not and people needed to get the message.

We doubled down in our efforts and with Qayden's help in July of 2014 we began doing the t-shirt experiment full time. This time we were armed with a new shirt that said "MONEY IS NOT REAL, I AM." Qayden unlike his brother and sisters didn't remember what things had been like before 2007. As a soon to be 4th grader he didn't have the same reservations that now plagued our other three children. And I am sure at this point they had had quite enough. The shirts definitely garnered a whole lot of attention and being stared at as a pre-teen and teen wasn't their idea of a good time. The kids had lived it and it had been hard especially for Qadira.

They longed for us to just be normal but we no longer had a concept of what that even was. And somehow over the years as we fought in the courts Qayden had developed out of nowhere a deep belief and commitment to the truth. He became our little rock. So many times during the fight just his conviction that "They" would not win because "They" did not have God on their side was enough kindling to throw onto the fire to keep us both going. It was a firm foundation.

We wore the shirts everyday now and the leadership was very displeased along with everyone else. In September of 2014 the Department of Justice sent a letter to the Ninth Circuit Court of Appeals wondering aloud when they would finally dismiss the big case. There was no answer. On Renee's appeal against Nike it was quiet. Everything was quiet until Renee went to renew his license and then all of a sudden it was some more bullshit. Now they claimed that he had given false information to the DMV in 1998. What was their evidence you ask? It was just a picture of his head photo-shopped onto his brother's body. And even though his brother signed an affidavit stating that it was in fact his body in the picture they still came after Renee.

The judge claimed that he had lied to the DMV back in 1998 so that he could appear to be 21 because I had been 21 at the time. What a load of crap. In between my pregnancy with Qadira, planning our wedding, and working fulltime at Adidas he hadn't had much time for anything else. But nobody would listen. And the mysterious "They" took his license anyway. By now we were used to their bullshit. And honestly it was exhausting. I was so tired.

And every day we continued to march around town with the message. Everyone we ran into got the message but they all turned their backs on it. It appeared that nobody wanted anybody to matter and it was heartbreaking to witness. We were considered more of a problem than a solution. The more we persevered the more we were hated. The harder we tried the more we were spit on and cursed by everyone we met.

We couldn't get any recognition or help. Unable to use the police department Renee couldn't report the DMV situation to anybody who would listen. Our lives were hard enough and this just made things that much harder. What was Renee supposed to do? Stand around and not work, not go anywhere? So now when he drove he tried to be as careful as possible. It was all he could do. It would be a full year until he would see his license again. Nothing made any sense. Everyone around us had lost their minds. If we let the people around us determine our self-worth then we would be digging ourselves an early grave. We lived in a society where everyone just valued the money and we didn't have much of that.

We tried to imagine an entire world full of happy and healthy people and we spent day and night thinking about ways to get there. We both felt that there were concrete actions that people could take every day to make our current environment better. It would just take a tremendous collective focus that required people from all walks of life to engage in one serious conversation. We felt "The t-shirt experiment" was a good first step. It was a way for people to literally and physically practice seeing one another as valuable. It was the only way the world made sense to us now. Every life had to matter if any life was going to matter.

But that was not the world we lived in. The world we lived in made no sense. And there was no real way to take a much needed break. No wonder no one was having any fun around here. People could only pretend to be having fun when in reality they were suffering just as much as we were. It was all just a show, a "game" and we all participated in it. There were high paid actors everywhere to create a distraction so big that the Human Race was now in the process of killing everything and everyone just to keep feeding the beast.

We got up every day and kept putting on the shirts. Renee and Qayden were doing okay but I felt like it was killing me. We all chose not to walk away from the truth but I bore the brunt of its blows facing off with people whenever I could and getting very vocal on social media. Nobody wanted to hear it coming from me. They flung their hatred and insults in my direction as fast as they could. Nobody really cared about us or what we had been through. Everything just felt so hard all of the time and people everywhere hated the message. I wanted to die some of the days but that just wasn't happening. I was exhausted all the way deep inside my bones.

There was always so much work to be done; at home, at work, with the kids, at the house, and on Facebook. I never had a chance to relax. Death was just another vacation I could not afford like everything else on the planet. It was always more drudgery, more work, and it all sucked because nobody really cared. Nobody had time to care. That's just how this place is set up. I was very unpopular and people who knew what I was up to kept their distance. Good friends who I had known for years blocked me and unfriended me for who I had become. It was very disheartening but each blow strengthened our resolve not to leave our children in such a cold ugly place.

Depression threatened to overwhelm me but God kept waking me up in the morning telling me I had to keep moving forward. Why no one could understand or hear the truth was a mystery to us but we knew that we had to keep doing the work until we died. Every hour, every minute, every second we were Pay It Forward. And In December of 2014 we decided to put the shirts up for sale on Zazzle hoping to find more leaders who were willing to help us spread the message but once again we got slapped in the face. We couldn't even sell one shirt. SLAP, KICK, PUNCH! That definitely hurt like hell. It was a scathing indictment of what people really thought of us and our movement. But there was nowhere for us to move but forward and we barely took notice on November 3rd, 2015 when Justice Anthony Kennedy of The United States Supreme Court dismissed once and for all Stephens vs. Nike.

And shortly thereafter in February of 2015, more determined than ever, we set up an official website declaring to the world that we were in fact The Messengers. It was clear that nobody else wanted the job. We had offered it to lots of people and they all said no and somebody had to keep doing it. We settled in for the long haul. We boldly handed out business cards and kept talking to people and I worked day and night to finish this book. But the harder we tried to promote the more suspicion we encountered. It was a very difficult uphill battle. But we had come to firmly believe that life was the value so we had to keep fighting. The message had worked its way into our blood. America had fallen into the wrong hands and we felt it was imperative that we continue to stand.

THE AFTERSHOCK

To the surprise of everyone around us and despite the ongoing lack of support the year 2018 found Renee, Qayden, and I still heavily involved in the T-Shirt Experiment. It had become almost a second skin at this point. It was now only on the rare occasion that someone would see us without a shirt. This action practiced daily at school and work had not generated even one small article in any newspaper and we certainly didn't sell any shirts.

We all felt strongly about continuing to spread the idea but we had resigned ourselves to graciously not forcing it on anybody. We had all had moments where we seriously had debated taking off the shirt. The last four years had taken their toll. Qayden was now an excellent student who no longer talked about God much. He had come to rely on his own work ethic and inner strength. This gave some real meaning to the words "I AM THE VALUE." Now an eighth grader it took some real guts to be standing alone in a middle school hallway. We had all come to really believe in what we were doing and it seemed irresponsible to just give it up.

But if this was the world that everyone was content with then we recognized and accepted our inability to interfere with that decision. The big case had been quietly dismissed by The Ninth Circuit on February 21st 2017. We lived without any kind of resolution. Our lives became fairly routine again. Renee had become a professional carpenter and although I had moved over to an agency, I was still a caregiver. Working with our hands helped keep us both focused and centered. It was honest work and we didn't complain.

It is said that time can heal all things and there is definitely some truth to that. Renee had finally reconnected with his family and his mother now lived with us. My brother Sala eventually found his footing and was able to manage a job at a pizza place and a small apartment. The small victories would have to be enough. Life had kept moving forward.

I was surprised when Qadira came to me in early March and announced that she now wanted her justice. She and Kamaya had watched the Larry Nassar trials and the triggers for Qadira had exploded. Larry Nassar was the USA gymnastics national team doctor who was eventually convicted for molesting the girls he was supposed to be taking care of. For the longest time she had just tried to forget what had happened but she now realized there are some things you cannot just move on from. She wanted real answers and she felt as an adult she was entitled to some.

I couldn't believe she was sitting next to me thanking me for all I had done. I vowed to help her. We called up some extended family and we decided to have her make a new report to the police in front a large group of family witnesses at Sunday dinner. It had been almost 11 years and still the night of April 12th 2007 remained a mystery. Because she had been an unrepresented minor during the entire circumstance she was still well within her statues for reporting abuse and we held out hope that she would be taken seriously once and for all. But of course it was just a circus all over again. The officers took the report and we were referred to a Sergeant Kevin Warren.

Sergeant Kevin Warren rudely and unabashedly informed Qadira over the phone that "nothing was going to be done about this" and a trip back to OHSU had them threatening to arrest me if we tried to ask any questions about medical records. We got the same response from Providence. The general consensus was that even though we hadn't talked about anything this had somehow all been litigated and we had lost. And apparently if you lose in a court of law you can't ever ask any questions about anything ever again.

Lieutenant Stephanie Lorenco played dumb and Amber Kinny with the Oregon District Attorney's office sounded like the head cheerleader in a bad high school drama. They all took the time to inform me that we were not in with the in crowd. This of course was the punishment for going after Nike and it was apparently permanent.

We held our breath when we finally sat down with a reporter from The Skanner. It was a black owned newspaper that I had contacted many times before. I was shocked when they agreed to meet with us. Their reporter listened to our story but that was the end of that. Nobody was going to trade the richest man in Oregon for a little brown carpenter with nothing to offer but a message that nobody wanted.

Qadira was quickly disillusioned by the nonsense and after just a couple of weeks she gave up. I tried to fire up the people by having them call the DA and request an investigation and that worked just enough to get us a meeting with the Senior Deputy District Attorney John Casalino where he listened with the intent to do nothing. They did just enough to give the public the idea we were being heard when in fact we were being more ignored than ever. It was a clever strategy and people quickly lost interest in Qadira's case.

When Jennifer and Sarah Hart drove their six black adopted children off a cliff Oregon department of Human Services was cast into the headlines as having woefully inadequate systems in place to protect children. I rolled my eyes as far up into the back of my head as they would go. Really?! And the news stations carried on and on about the case as if something were really going to be done to fix the system. It was nothing but lip service. If they were serious about confronting the real issues they would come and sort things out with us.

And suddenly out of nowhere Nike was also cast into the cross hairs. A mass exodus of senior employees over allegations of a toxic workplace environment had the company turned upside down. A group of women had banded together and circulated a secret survey that had produced shocking results. Apparently there was an undisputed pattern of harassment and unchecked discrimination flowing through the company. We of course were not surprised. The apologies were flowing but none of them were coming in our direction. I had to sit there watching Mark Parker and Phil Knight pretending they were so shocked to hear the news. And of course I had to watch the media play along as if we did not exist.

America was firmly entrenched in the idea that confronting our failed system was optional and people all over the world suffered because of this decision. Phil Knight had originally wanted to call

Nike; "Dimension 6" and somehow the company had successfully
led the global community there. It was a dark place where wealthy
individuals were worth more than all of the blood spilt building this
nation. The freedom in America had been sold and with it all the
souls who had fought and died to make that dream a reality. It was
now up to every individual who ever loved this country to stand up
and help take those souls back. Our shirts alone were not enough
protection to withstand the heat that was burning the country to the
ground.

America was at a pivotal crossroad. Donald Trump had won the
leading role of President, we were on the eve of World War III, and
everyone was more determined than ever to keep the teakettle under
the rug. In all, we had filed 6 EEOC complaints, 6 lawsuits, and
multiple appeals. The action of pursuing our rights had caused us to
be completely stripped of them. We were no longer a nation of laws.
We were a nation on fire. And when Nike made Colin Kaepernick
the face of its new social justice campaign he quickly became their 6
billion dollar "profit" and we watched as America got down on its
knees. Was it possible that these three 6's had awakened The Beast?

I am one of 6 kids. There are 6 people in Renee's family, there are
6 people in our family, and it had taken us 6 years to get the message.
Now, 6 years after that, I was finally publishing this book. The
summer of the year 2019 would also be the beginning of the 6th year
of the t-shirt experiment-- 666. That pesky little number had become
a huge pain in my ass. There were literally 6's everywhere. We even
currently owned 6 old cars that were taking up all the parking space
all around our house. It was beginning to look like more than a
coincidence.

From its location in Beaverton, Nike was just a stone's throw
away from The Pacific Ocean. The largest and deepest of the Earth's
oceanic divisions the deep abyss is also home to the treacherous Ring
of Fire which contains 452 volcanoes. About 90 percent of the
world's earthquakes occur along the Ring of Fire. Stephens vs. Nike
could be likened to an earthquake and a volcanic eruption. Renee's
initial complaint had caused the Shoe Giant to release a tsunami of
hatred and uncontrollable anger, which then caused an eruption that
produced a burning stream that left an open wound that could not be
healed, and a lasting mark that could not be denied.

The courts certainly had given Nike power and authority over

America by allowing the company to circumvent every single allegation we had thrown in their direction. By disregarding their own process the judges had inadvertently fed the growing giant and now it could not be contained. The new campaign had turned Nike into a political powerhouse with a religious fervor that was quickly sweeping the nation.

A great blasphemy was being disseminated and people were buying it left and right. Nike had hung its new "prophet" out for the whole world to see with the words "believe in something even if it means sacrificing everything" scrawled across his face. It was the new mantra that was everywhere making my ears bleed. The right to play a game for obscene "profits" was being served and I now found it virtually impossible to avoid tripping over the new morally superior swoosh

Now if you did not worship Nike the progressive masses were ready to hang you from a cross. The company sales were up 31 percent as people were now "branding" themselves with the logo to show how much they cared about social justice. We had been shoved into a dark hole and Phil had thrown away the key. A new King had been crowned and like an eagle he had made sure to rip all the flesh from my bones. Like an ox I had pounded on the door until my fists bled and like a ghost my cries could not be heard.

The Shoe Giant had now morphed into The Beast. We had delivered a fatal wound directly to its head but it had been magically healed by the power of The Almighty Dollar. Like a leopard no one heard it coming and like a bear its large feet and long claws had thwarted every action we had directed towards it. Nike was the lion who sat on the throne and the dragon who protected it breathed the fire of poverty at anyone who dared cross its path.

The corporation was the jewel of the world and on its head was the 10 crowns of the world's wealthiest nations with 10 horns ready to gut anything that stood in its way. People on all 7 continents stood ready to defend the Beast's honor. In their right hand was the money and branded into their forehead was the idea that it was the only thing that mattered. Without both, then the right to buy or sell became impossible. This wasn't a very nice game but everyone was determined to keep playing it.

I popped a bag of popcorn and waited patiently for Barack Obama to reemerge. And on September 7th 2018, true to form, there he was lecturing me and everyone else all over again. Apparently, "that guy" was never going to find his way home. The price of everything was set to go up until only a few could breathe. And finally on October 6th 2018 Portland, Oregon welcomed the Pharaoh to the Oregon Museum of Science and Industry.

At this point we had literally been fined thousands for simply complaining about anything. The "artifacts" that were supposed to be shared equally were not to be touched. Nike had really done a little "number" on this place. The Goddess of victory had won. This isn't a free country. This is the Pharaoh's tomb, where "The Bill Of Rights" is preserved neatly under thick glass for use only by the rich and powerful. The United States of America had been officially swooshed.

ABOUT THE AUTHOR

Karellen Stephens is the mother of four children and a caregiver for the elderly. She is married to Renee Stephens and is the co-founder of and Chief Activist at Justice for Qadira and the co-founder of Pay It Forward Leadership Society. She lives in Portland, Oregon and she spends all of her spare time trying to change the world.

Made in USA - Kendallville, IN
1213207_9798577075651
12.15.2020 0825